OUTDOOR STRUCTURES

HOME REPAIR
AND IMPROVEMENT

OUTDOOR STRUCTURES

BY THE EDITORS OF
TIME-LIFE BOOKS

TIME-LIFE BOOKS
ALEXANDRIA, VIRGINIA

HOME REPAIR AND IMPROVEMENT

Editor	William Frankel
Designer	Anne Masters

Editorial Staff for Outdoor Structures

Picture Editor	Adrian G. Allen
Text Editors	Stuart Gannes, William H. Forbis, John Manners, Brian McGinn, Bob Menaker, Ellen Phillips
Writers	Megan Barnett, Thierry Bright-Sagnier, Stephen Brown, Alan Epstein, Steven J. Forbis, Lydia Preston, Brooke C. Stoddard, David Thiemann
Assistant Designer	Kenneth E. Hancock
Copy Coordinator	Margery duMond
Art Assistants	George Bell, Mary Louise Mooney, Lorraine D. Rivard, Richard Whiting
Picture Coordinator	Renée DeSandies
Editorial Assistant	Susanne S. Trice

Editorial Operations

Production Director	Feliciano Madrid
Assistants	Peter A. Inchauteguiz, Karen A. Meyerson
Copy Processing	Gordon E. Buck
Quality Control Director	Robert L. Young
Assistant	James J. Cox
Associates	Daniel J. McSweeney, Michael G. Wight
Art Coordinator	Anne B. Landry
Copy Room Director	Susan Galloway Goldberg
Assistants	Celia Beattie, Ricki Tarlow

Correspondents: Elisabeth Kraemer (Bonn); Margot Hapgood, Dorothy Bacon, Lesley Coleman (London); Susan Jonas, Lucy T. Voulgaris (New York); Maria Vincenza Aloisi, Josephine du Brusle (Paris); Ann Natanson (Rome). Valuable assistance was also provided by: Judy Aspinall, Karin B. Pearce (London); Carolyn T. Chubet, Miriam Hsia, Christina Lieberman (New York); Mimi Murphy (Rome).

THE CONSULTANTS: James H. Pendleton, general consultant for this book, is construction superintendent and chief landscape designer for a nursery in northern Virginia. His work has been exhibited at the Washington, D.C., Armory Flower Show.

Harris Mitchell, special consultant for Canada, has worked in the field of home repair and improvement since 1950. He is Homes editor of *Today* magazine, writes a syndicated newspaper column, "You Wanted to Know," and is the author of a number of books on home improvement.

Roswell W. Ard, a civil engineer, is a consulting structural engineer and a professional home inspector.

For information about any Time-Life book, please write:
Reader Information
Time-Life Books
541 North Fairbanks Court
Chicago, Illinois 60611

Library of Congress Cataloguing in Publication Data
Time-Life Books.
    Outdoor structures.
    (Home repair and improvement; v. 13)
    Includes index.
    1. Building—Amateurs' manuals. I. Title.
TH4955.T55   1978   690'.8'9   78-1110
ISBN 0-8094-2404-5
ISBN 0-8094-2403-7 (lib. bdg.)
ISBN 0-8094-2402-9 (retail ed.)

Contents

1

Laying the Groundwork

Whatever the shape, size or conformation of the land around your house, you can probably improve both its looks and its utility by adding a few easy-to-build yet sturdy and handsome outdoor structures. Toolsheds and garages protect belongings; shade houses, gazebos and garden ponds add comfort and charm. Fences and walls not only ensure privacy and define boundaries but, with artful geometry, provide attractive backdrops and, through skillful placement, moderate the force of the wind and the flow of frost.

The land itself can be remolded to create more pleasing contours, to improve drainage, to halt erosion or to prepare the way for the foundation of an outdoor structure. Most such construction starts with either leveling or excavating—or both—and may even involve a little surveying, a fascinating and easily mastered technique. Earth-moving requires a fairly intimate knowledge of both the surface and the subsurface of the property. Before you start building, find out whether local building and zoning codes dictate drainage patterns, fence heights or road easements. In any case, property lines, septic tanks and underground power, water and gas lines always must be marked out before any excavation work begins. In many regions of the country, utility companies will stake out the locations of their lines and pipes on request and free of charge, while county engineers will conduct soil tests to ensure that the ground is strong and stable enough to support a planned structure.

The techniques and materials described in this book are not as complex or as costly as those used on a home. The exterior concrete slabs shown here, for example, are reinforced with steel mesh, but in most cases they are thinner than one poured for a house, and many light structures can rest on precast piers or, like greenhouses and fence posts, may be set directly in or on top of the soil.

The structures themselves are similarly simple to construct. Many are open, designed to direct and encourage a pleasing flow of light and air. For such buildings, an unusual variety of construction techniques is available: post-and-beam, for example, allows the builder to use 4- to 8-inch-thick members that can bear tremendous loads and are spaced at greater intervals and with somewhat less precision than is found in residential framing. A-framing, where walls and roofs are identical, is also convenient, while domes, built like bubbles without interior bracing, are ideal for areas where posts, beams and studs would be impossible or undesirable to use. When you are building relatively small, open structures, these methods eliminate the need for costly framing materials and for the advanced carpentry skills and precision workmanship required for homebuilding. They make buildings that any amateur can put up—and be proud of.

Surveying Property with Speed and Precision

The property lines that define the boundaries of a plot of land are seldom visible, but a landowner has to know where his property begins and ends when he plans an outdoor structure that could trespass on neighboring land. To find his boundaries, the landowner must use the findings of the professional surveyors who originally established and staked out the dimensions of his property.

The dimensions determined by the surveyors are marked on the lot plat, or map, that is generally furnished with the title to the land and is kept on file at a local courthouse or record office. When mapping the land, the surveyors also drive stakes, usually made of metal, into the ground at the corners of the plot to serve as property markers. These stakes may be lost in undergrowth or buried beneath a few inches of earth. But if they are metal, and as long as you can locate one of them, your property map and a little basic geometry will enable you to find the others. And with all the markers located, you can determine the boundaries by driving stakes next to the markers, then stretching string between the stakes.

Once the boundaries are established, a few simple surveying techniques and tools will enable you to map the location and size of the structure you want to build. Distances can be measured fairly accurately with string, wooden stakes, a carpenter's tape measure and a roll of light-gauge tie wire, available at hardware stores. A professional water level or a water-filled length of transparent garden hose makes a precise tool for determining heights or slopes and establishing level points; when exact measurements are not essential, an inexpensive line level will serve the same purpose.

Some jobs, however, call for a degree of accuracy that can be attained only with specialized surveying instruments.

To measure exact vertical and horizontal angles, to sight lines for pouring foundations, or to establish perfect parallels to property lines, you should use a transit level, a telescope-like device with which builders, engineers and surveyors perform a variety of measuring tasks quickly and very precisely. Transit levels can be rented from surveying firms and, like any precision tool, they must be handled carefully. Do not, for example, use one on an excessively damp day: moisture can affect the accuracy of the readings on the instrument.

Caution: any measurement, no matter how carefully taken, is only an approximation and even official surveys may not be totally accurate. To avoid the possibility of accidentally infringing upon a neighbor's land, always stay at least 12 inches within the boundaries of your property when you are planning the location of any outdoor structure.

Finding Property Markers

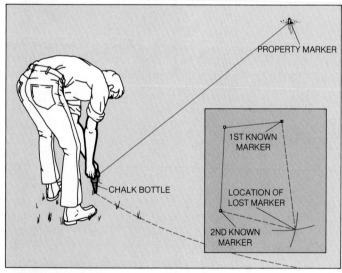

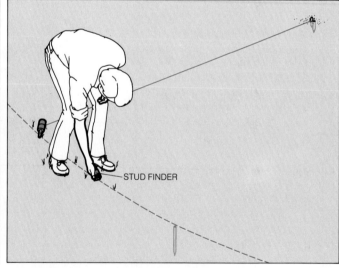

Using two adjacent markers. Drive a wooden stake next to an established marker, attach a length of tie wire equal to the distance between the established and the lost marker (as indicated on your property map) and swing the other end of the wire in an arc, using powdered chalk to trace the arc on the ground. Drive a stake at a second known marker and repeat the procedure, using a length of wire equal to the distance between the second marker and the missing one. Where the two chalked arcs cross (*inset*), locate the lost marker by digging.

From a single reference marker. Using your property map and a tie wire to establish a point at the correct distance and direction from the marker, swing the end of the wire to run a chalk arc on the ground and walk a stud finder along the arc. When the stud finder's magnetic needle deflects, dig for the marker. If the stud finder fails to deflect, then metal markers may be sunk too deeply, or else the markers are made of wood. In that case you will need to locate at least two visible markers or call a professional surveyor to reestablish the property lines.

Simple Sighting and Leveling Techniques

Sighting a straight line. To establish a straight line to an unseen location—in this example, a point on the other side of a hill—drive stakes at both the starting and the unseen point. Stand at one stake, station a helper at the other and have two more helpers hold tall poles in between, at points where the tops of the poles can be seen from both stake positions *(below, top)*. Sighting from your stake, signal the polemen to move until their poles are in a straight line of sight from your position. Have the polemen turn around *(below, bottom)*, let the other sighter move them until their poles form a straight line from his position, then alternate sightings until the poles appear in line from both positions *(below, insets)*. Connect all four points with a string.

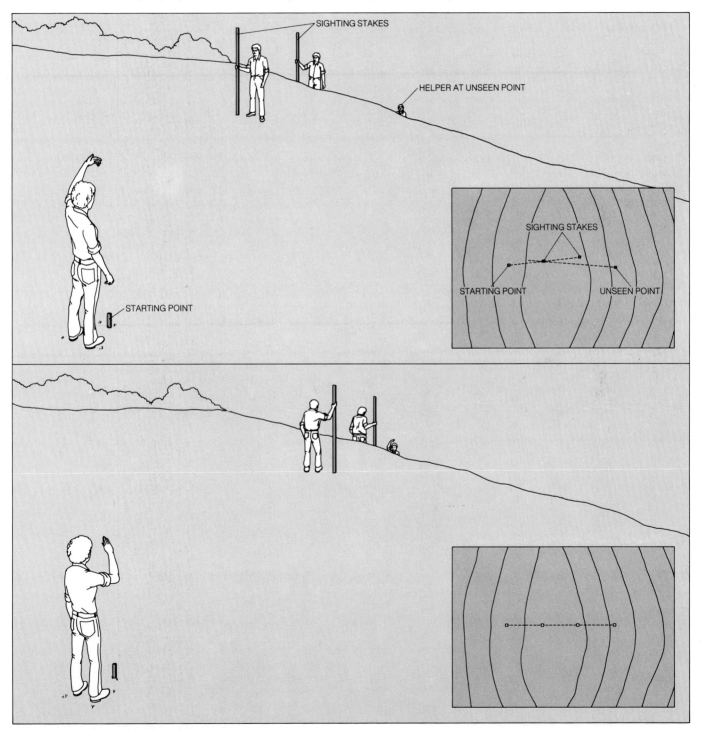

SIGHTING STAKES

HELPER AT UNSEEN POINT

STARTING POINT

SIGHTING STAKES

STARTING POINT   UNSEEN POINT

Finding levels over uneven surfaces. Use a water level or a transparent plastic hose partly filled with water to find on one stake or post a point that is exactly level with a mark on another. Stretch the hose between the stakes, hold one end a few inches above the mark you have made and have a helper hold the other end at about the same height. Using a funnel, fill the hose with water until the level reaches the mark. Make sure there are no air bubbles—if there are, pour off the water and refill the hose—then mark the second stake at the water level in the hose.

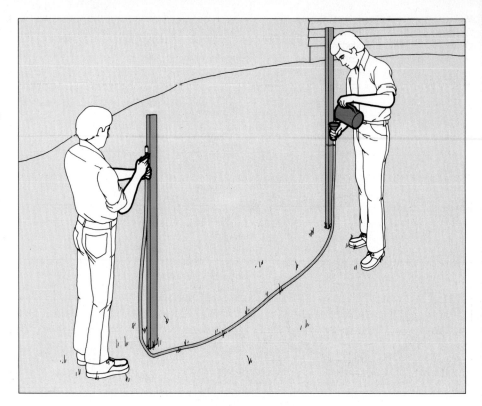

A Telescope that Measures Angles

Anatomy of a transit level. This professional surveying tool is essentially a tripod-mounted movable telescope with precise scales for vertical and horizontal angles. The 20-power telescope pivots at its center for vertical measurements and the entire mounting carriage rotates on the undercarriage for horizontal ones. To enable you to check the instrument for level and plumb, a small spirit level is mounted under the telescope and a hook for a plumb bob hangs from the base plate; the undercarriage slides over the base plate to position the bob, and four leveling screws are used to set the level.

Angles are measured on horizontal and vertical scales; when only horizontal measurements are needed, a pair of levers locks the telescope in the level position. Cross hairs in the telescope are focused by turning the eyepiece, and should only have to be set once; the focusing wheel provides a fine adjustment. For precise aiming, use the slow-motion screws to turn the telescope, and lock it in position with corresponding clamp screws.

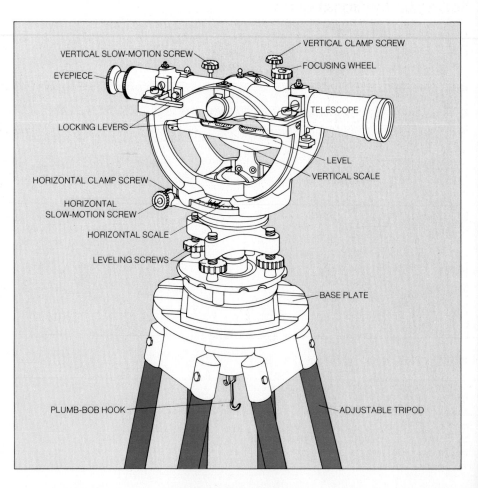

VERTICAL SLOW-MOTION SCREW
VERTICAL CLAMP SCREW
EYEPIECE
FOCUSING WHEEL
TELESCOPE
LOCKING LEVERS
LEVEL
VERTICAL SCALE
HORIZONTAL CLAMP SCREW
HORIZONTAL SLOW-MOTION SCREW
HORIZONTAL SCALE
LEVELING SCREWS
BASE PLATE
PLUMB-BOB HOOK
ADJUSTABLE TRIPOD

Measuring angles to the nearest degree. Vertical angles are read on a 90° arc, horizontal angles on a circular scale divided into four 90° arcs; small auxiliary scales called verniers serve as pointers for the main scales and give readings in sixtieths of a degree, or minutes.

To measure a horizontal angle between two points to the nearest degree, focus the telescope on the first point and note the reading on the main scale closest to the zero mark on the vernier.

Swing the telescope to the second point and note the new reading. If both readings fall within the same 90° arc, subtract the first reading from the second. If the readings fall on adjoining arcs, follow these rules: when the arcs are separated by a zero, add the readings; when the arcs are separated by the figure 90, add the readings and subtract the total from 180.

Vertical angles up to 40° are measured above and below level, indicated by a zero.

Measuring fractions of an angle. If the zero mark on the vernier falls between two degree marks on the main scale, read the lower mark and use the vernier to calculate the fraction in minutes. Reading upward from the degree mark, find the mark on the vernier that coincides with a main-scale mark. Count the vernier spaces between the two main-scale marks. Each space stands for five minutes; multiply the number of spaces by five to get a reading in minutes. The sighting below reads 17° 15′.

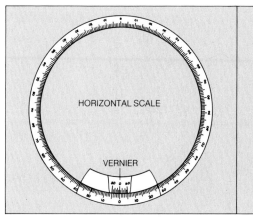

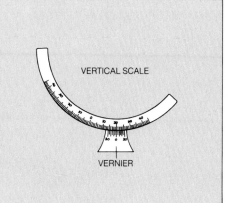

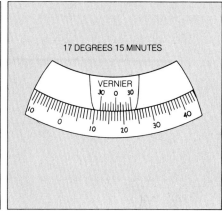

Setting Up the Transit Level

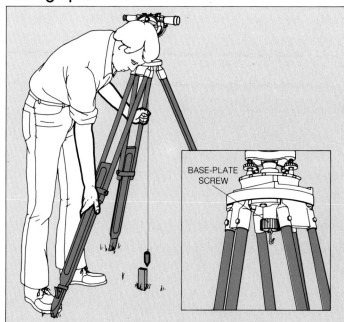

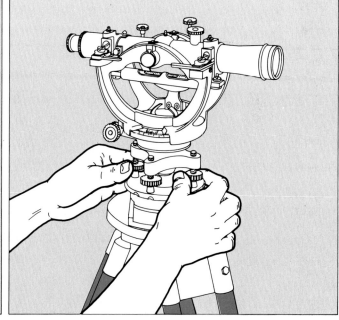

Plumbing the tripod. Spread the tripod legs 3 feet apart over a stake or other marker used as a sighting point and move the legs one at a time until the plumb bob hangs no more than ¼ inch horizontally from the center of the stake. Loosen the screw under the base plate and shift the transit level on the base plate until the plumb bob hangs directly over the center of the stake. Tighten the base-plate screw.

Leveling the transit. Loosen two adjacent leveling screws and turn the telescope until it aligns with two opposite leveling screws, then turn these opposite screws slowly until the bubble in the level is centered. Rotate the telescope 90° to align it with the other pair of opposite screws and repeat the procedure. Adjust opposite screws until the bubble in the level remains centered as the telescope swings full circle.

Getting Lines and Angles Exactly Right

Setting a straight line. Drive stakes at the two points to be aligned. Set up the transit over the starting stake with its locking levers open, focus on the other stake by using the cross hairs and tighten the horizontal clamp screw. Have a helper hold a stake at the approximate position of the next-to-last stake, lower the telescope and have the helper move his stake until you can focus on it; have him drive down the stake. Repeat the procedure for the other stakes.

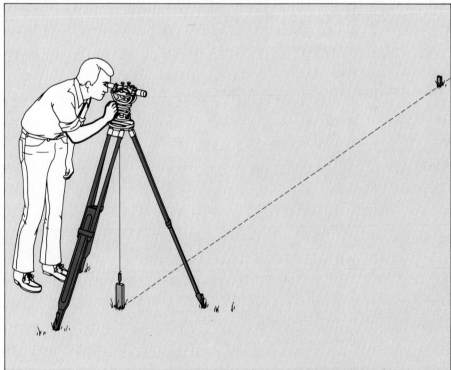

Setting a right angle. Set a straight line to a stake, then rotate the transit level exactly 90° on the horizontal scale and use the horizontal clamp screw to lock it in position. Have a helper move another stake until you can sight it in the cross hairs, then have him drive this stake in place. Check the angle by swinging the transit level back 90° to the original stake.

How to Sight around an Obstruction

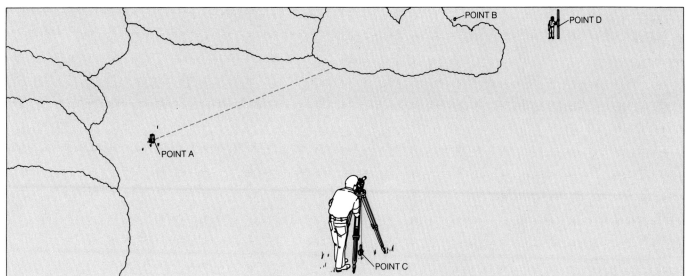

1 **Plotting an approximate parallel.** You will sometimes have to set a straight line parallel to a line that is obstructed, such as a property line running between points A and B in the example above. Set up the transit over a starting stake where the view is unobstructed—point C in this example—and sight a line approximately parallel to line A-B. On this line, drive a stake at point D so that lines A-B and C-D are equal. Stretch tie wire between points C and D.

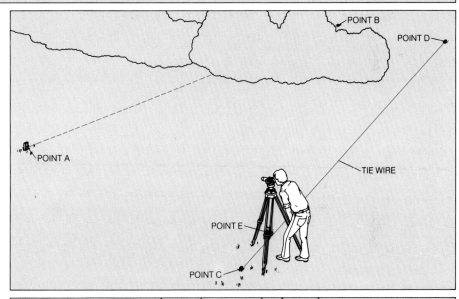

2 **Locating the first stake.** From point C, rotate the transit 90° toward point A, and move the instrument along the line of tie wire until the cross hairs align with the stake at point A. Double-check the sighting by rotating the transit 90° toward point D; the cross hairs should align with the stake at D. Drive a stake directly underneath the transit (at point E), measure the distance between points A and E, and cut a length of tie wire equal to that distance.

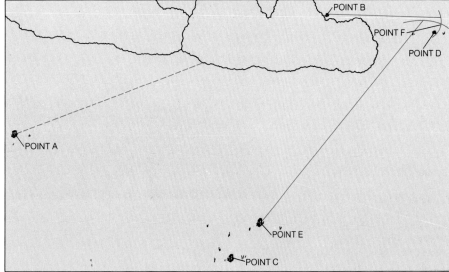

3 **Locating the second stake.** Attach the length of tie wire to the stake at point B and swing it in an arc toward point D as shown on page 8. Loosen the tie wire joining points C and D, fasten one end to the stake at point E and swing the other end in an arc toward point D. Plant a stake where the two arcs intersect (point F). The line joining points E and F is now parallel to the property line between points A and B.

Your Land Reshaped to Suit Your Needs

Flattening a stretch of land, creating subtle drainage gradients, controlling the runoff of surface water—these necessary grading jobs may sound vague and ambitious. They become exact and easy when you use the professional earth-molding techniques shown on the following pages. Moreover, you can do most of the work with plain hand tools.

Grades, which are areas smoothed and sloped for drainage, are made in two types. In one type a pair of fixed points, such as the street and the garage entrance at the opposite ends of a driveway, determine the slope. In the other, the surface of the ground is sloped just enough to drain off excess rain water, as may be necessary in a formal lawn, a patio or a setting for a garden house.

To set a grade having two fixed points, you must begin by measuring the difference in elevation—that is, the rise—between the points. The preferred ratio of the rise to the horizontal distance between the points varies, from 1 foot for every 10 feet of an entrance walk to 1 foot for every 7 feet of a driveway, and a

maximum of 1 foot for every 3 feet of a grassy bank. If you find that the grade is too steep, you must build a solution into the site—adding steps to a walk, for example, or building a retaining wall for a lawn. For a grade as nearly level as possible, the standard minimum is 1 inch of rise for each 4 feet of horizontal run (in porous soil where drainage is less of a problem, ½ inch is enough).

You can make these minimal grades by the string-grid method shown in these pages. The grid can also establish an exact plane for a slope between fixed points—for example, a driveway. But you can dispense with the grid in grading a lawn between such fixed points as a foundation and a sidewalk, if the land has a slope of 6 inches or more in each 4 feet of run. In this situation your eye and your judgment will serve to make the grade sufficiently flat.

Grades are the major factor in the drainage of your property, and establishing grades that drain well must take priority over the cosmetics of landscaping. But professional land-shapers use other

ways to drain land—by slowing fast runoff, by diverting water from areas that are especially vulnerable to water damage and by draining water from any area in which it tends to collect.

Use a double-ended pick with a point and a mattock to loosen earth for grading and draining. A plain pointed shovel with a long handle serves best for the digging. If you buy or rent a wheelbarrow for the job, get one with pneumatic tires and an oak frame. Rotary tillers with rear tines, available at tool-rental agencies, are comparatively expensive, but they till better and can be guided more easily than front-tine machines.

The fastest and easiest way to compact land is to roll it in two directions with a roller. But a roller is not sufficient if you have to fill; you must tamp the earth with a hand tamper or a power-driven machine tamper after putting down each 4- to 6-inch layer of soil or gravel. You must also tamp down the bottoms of swales, the slopes and tops of terraces and any area of soil that will lie under a concrete slab or a layer of gravel.

Making a Smooth and Sloping Grade

1 Establishing a rough grade. With a pick and shovel, cut down all mounds and ridges, moving the dirt into holes and valleys. If the slope runs in a direction different from the planned grade, use a wheelbarrow to move dirt from the high side to the planned new high side. As you work, either bury debris such as weeds, wood scraps and stones in a hole or pile it up to be carted away later. When you have finished, the grade should look approximately flat.

2 Tilling the soil. Use a rotary tiller to break up clods and make the soil easy to rake. Set the machine for deep tilling and till back and forth across the width and the length of the plot, making tight turns by releasing the drive clutch and swinging the tiller around on its wheels (or, for a front-tine tiller, on its tines).

3 Setting the slope of the grade. Drive stakes at the corners of the area to be graded. At one of the upper stakes tie a string 6 inches above the planned high edge of the grade, stretch the string to the lower stake on the same side and level it with a line level; mark the lower stake at the string. For a minimal grade, as in this example, measure 1 inch down from the mark for each 4 feet of string, and tie the string at that point. Tie level strings, from the first string to the stakes on the other side of the area, and complete the boundary with a fourth string. For a grade with two fixed points, dispense with the line level: tie the first string to the upper and lower stakes 6 inches above the fixed points, then complete the boundary.

To measure the rise of a grade for planning purposes, tie the string at ground level on a stake at the area's upper edge and measure directly from the string to the ground at the lower edge.

4 **Making a grid.** Drive stakes at 6-foot intervals along the boundary strings and connect each opposite pair of stakes with string to make a grid. If any grid string touches the ground, scoop out the earth beneath it to form a trench.

5 **Establishing the finish grade.** Working under and between the strings, use a shovel and a rake to move the soil into a flat surface parallel to the plane of the grid; judge by eye to see that the middle of each 6-foot square is level with the sides under the strings. Add or remove soil as needed to bring the grade exactly to the planned height, then turn the rake tines up and use the back of the tool to finish-smooth the surface. Remove the strings and stakes and compact the soil by either rolling or tamping, depending on the function of the graded area.

Halting Erosion and Improving Drainage

Generally, the problems of surface drainage on a house lot have three causes: erosion, grades that direct runoff in an undesirable direction, and boggy low spots that accumulate water. Grading can solve problems, but the topography or the amount of earth to be moved may make this solution impractical. However, in most cases there are solutions that do not call for extensive grading.

The easiest way to stop erosion is to slow the velocity of the runoff. One technique for doing so is to install baffles, such as the buried railroad ties shown at right. Baffles block descending surface water before it gains much speed; the water flows over a baffle and renews its run, only to hit another baffle. The baffles are set in the ground on a slight gradient, end to end, so that they will not hold water after a rain stops. And if the baffles are obtrusive and unsightly, they can be concealed with plantings.

Another technique for slowing the velocity of runoff water is to build a terrace without a retaining wall (right, below). Here, the water descending a short steep slope is stopped by the terrace before it can run fast enough to erode the soil. Terraces look better than baffles, but they take more labor to construct.

To stop runoff toward some vulnerable feature of a property, such as a patio, a mound for decorative planting, or a house foundation (where accumulations of water can cause basement flooding), the specific solution is an interceptor ditch called a swale. Located and shaped so as to be nearly invisible, the swale carries surface water sideways and diverts it around the object or away from the area to be protected.

The problem of standing water in depressions can be cured in two ways. One is the straightforward method of filling the hole. The other consists of draining the water into a dry well; it seeps away through the sides and bottom of the well. Where possible, connect the dry well by installing a drainpipe to a lower part of the land or to a storm sewer located on your property.

Slowing runoff with baffles. Across the face of a slope, dig trenches in an open zigzag pattern, making each trench deep enough to bury all but 2 inches of railroad ties or 6-by-6 timbers. Use a line level (page 15, Step 3) to give the trenches an end-to-end gradient of 1 inch for each 4 feet of length and start the high end of every course about 6 inches beyond the bottom of the course above, to make it catch end spillage from the course above. Pin the timbers to the ground (page 22, Step 2). Caution: wear gloves when handling creosoted railroad ties.

Slowing runoff with a terrace. Drive stakes about 18 inches vertically above the foot of the slope at one end of the planned terrace, stretch a level string across the slope and mark the ground along the string with chalk from a squeeze bottle; then dig into the slope above the mark and deposit the soil below it. Keep the dropoff of the filled part at the angle at which the soil falls naturally and shape the dropoff in the cut part to the same angle. Form the flat part of the terrace so that a basketball placed in it will roll slowly to the dropoff.

Channeling water with a swale. Above and to the sides of the object or area to be protected from runoff, dig trenches as wide as a shovel, with sides that slant upward at a low angle and meet in the middle. Adjust the depth of the trenches to the steepness of the natural slope—from 2 inches deep for a slope of 1 foot of rise to 6 feet of run, to 5 inches deep for a slope of 1 to 2. Throw the soil you remove about 18 inches downhill to form a low dam, called a berm; shave the upper shoulder of the trench back about 18 inches, adding this soil to the berm; then shave the lower shoulder back to the berm (*inset*). Tamp the swale and test its internal slope by rolling a basketball down it.

Excavating a Dry Well

1 Digging a hole. After deciding on the size of the dry well, dig the hole for it in the lowest part of the depression. Starting from the hole, dig a trench 18 inches below the surface, dropping at a slope of 1 inch in 4 feet to a lower part of your property (*right*). Install 4-inch perforated plastic drain tile in the trench, covering the ends of the tile with fiberglass cloth to prevent them from filling with dirt. Then refill the trench.

2 **Installing gravel for drainage.** Line the hole with 1-inch fiberglass insulation, fastened to the sides of the hole with sixpenny galvanized nails, and fill the hole with gravel to a level 8 inches below the surface. Cover the gravel with fiberglass and the fiberglass with soil.

Relocating a Recalcitrant Rock

Not often, but too often, a homeowner moving soil on his property hears his pick strike solid rock. Exploring further, he discovers that the soil conceals a large boulder exactly where the putting green or the garage foundation was to go. He may be happy to know that his property contains some big stones suitable for a rock garden—but the stone must be moved.

Any rounded stone bigger than 30 inches in its longest dimension weighs upwards of 300 pounds. In most cases a professional should move it, using a backhoe or a front-end loader. Even in dealing with smaller stones, you have to consider the dangers of back strain and loss of control. One simple way to get a large protruding rock out of your way—in relatively rock-free soil—is to dig a deep hole alongside it, and lever the rock down into the excavation. But if you feel confident of your muscles and

prudence, you can move a stone measuring 30 inches or less with prybars and a makeshift wooden dolly. First, remove the soil around a deeply buried stone and dig a ramp to the surface. Then lever the stone onto a piece of heavy burlap, wrap the burlap around it and form the edges of the burlap into handholds. With a helper or two, skid the stone out of the hole.

Make the dolly from a 4-foot square piece of ¾-inch plywood laid on top of four lengths of 4-inch plastic drainpipe set about 14 inches apart. With a plank ramp, skid the stone to the middle of the plywood. Using the pipes as rollers, push the stone along the ground until the rear pipe is free of the trailing edge. Place this pipe ahead of the dolly and push again, repeating the process until the stone is just short of its destination, then tilt the plywood to slide the stone to the ground.

How to Terrace Slopes with Retaining Walls

For centuries farmers have turned steep hillsides into cultivable land. The technique is simple—they build an ascending series of retaining walls up a slope and fill the areas behind the walls with fertile soil until the ground is level. The same technique will serve to turn a sloping yard into a series of patios or gardens. Though most retaining walls are now built of timber, which is easier to work with and maintain than the traditional fieldstone of the farmer's wall, the principles of construction remain the same.

Because earth and water create tremendous pressures behind a retaining wall, you must make your wall strong and provide for adequate drainage. Begin your planning by checking local regulations on drainage (any change in the contour of your land affects the flow of water across it). In many localities a building inspector will examine your initial layout and make recommendations for drainage routes. For a wall more than 3 feet high, you will probably need a building permit, and may have to submit plans drawn up by a structural engineer.

The next stage of planning deals with the materials you will use. For the walls themselves, you can choose between railroad ties and pressure-treated lumber. The ties are inexpensive but they are soaked with creosote, which will quickly dull the blade of a chain saw and is poisonous to many plants. Redwood, which is handsome and naturally resists moisture, is perhaps the most popular wood for outdoor structures but is expensive. As a compromise, consider poplar or pine timbers, pressure treated with harmless preservatives, as durable as redwood and much cheaper. They come in 6-by-6 or 6-by-8 sizes; choose 8-foot lengths, the easiest to work with.

At the same time, decide upon the grade of lumber to order. Finish grade, the most expensive, comes with edges neatly planed and ends perfectly square so that you need not square the ends of every timber before butting it to its neighbor; less expensive grades make more work but save money. Whatever grade you choose, buy 20 per cent more timber than your calculations indicate as a minimum amount, to allow for waste. An 8-foot timber weighs from 100 to 200 pounds; save yourself labor by planning access routes so that the lumberyard can stack your wood close to your job site.

At the same time, lay out routes for a gravel company's delivery of drainage gravel and backfill, to be delivered sometime after you have completed the construction of the wall. The gravel company will advise you on the best fill for your purposes; if you are planning gardens or lawns, buy shredded topsoil and mulch for the top 6 inches of fill. To determine how much fill you will need, calculate the volume of fill in cubic yards—the length of a wall (in feet) times its height times the distance from its base to the next wall. Divide the answer in half (because approximately half the space behind the wall is already filled with existing soil), then divide the result by 27, to convert cubic feet to cubic yards. Finally, add 20 per cent to allow for compaction. For a drainage bed, order a ton of clean 1-inch gravel for each 25 feet of wall.

Beyond common household tools, you will need a chain saw (page 23) and a heavy-duty drill fitted with a ⅜-inch electrician's ship-auger bit 18 inches long. Anchor the wall to the hillside with three 42-inch lengths of ⅜-inch reinforcing steel—commonly called rebar—for every 8 feet of wall, and peg the layers of timbers together with three 12-inch pieces of ⅜-inch rebar for every 8 feet of wall.

Anatomy of a retaining wall. Two timber retaining walls, each 3 feet high, terrace this hillside. Each wall consists of seven courses of 6-by-6-inch lumber. The first course, buried in a trench 6 inches deep, is anchored to the hillside by 42-inch spikes made of ⅜-inch reinforcing steel. Succeeding courses are pinned together with 12-inch vertical spikes, and overlapping timbers are spiked horizontally and vertically.

To help the wall withstand the pressure of the compacted earth behind it, each course is set ¼ inch closer to the hillside than the one below, and angled into the hill. Eight-foot reinforcing timbers called deadmen run back from the wall at 6-foot intervals, and the free end of each deadman is attached to a crossplate spiked to the earth. As a final brace, side walls are built up on the outermost deadmen and connected to the retaining wall by interlocked corners.

To prevent water from building up behind the wall, the timbers in the second course are separated by 1-inch drainage gaps. In addition, 4-inch perforated drain tile buried in gravel routes water beyond the ends of the wall.

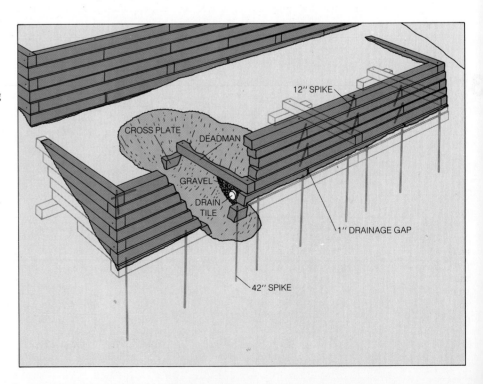

Preparing the Site

1 Marking the wall trench. Drive 5-foot stakes at the points you have chosen for the corners and tie a line between the stakes, using a water level to make sure it is horizontal *(page 10)*; then measure down from the line to find the point where the line is highest above ground—the "lowest grade point." Mark this point with a stake.

Adjust the line between the corner stakes so that it is 3 feet above the ground at the lowest grade point. Drop a plumb line every 4 feet along this line and drive stakes at these points to mark the outer edge of the wall. String a second line along the lower stakes.

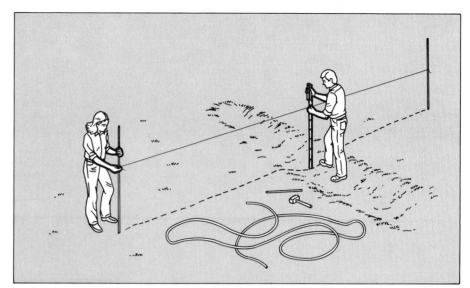

2 Laying out a terrace. From the 3-foot mark on a corner stake, stretch a line into the hillside and level it with a line level, then drive a 5-foot stake where the line meets the ground. Measure the distance between the two stakes along the ground and drive a 5-foot stake at this distance from the other corner stake.

Use the two uphill stakes to establish the height of a second retaining wall.

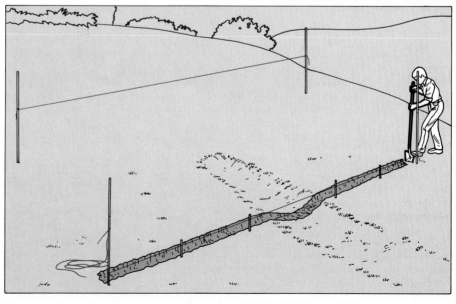

LINE LEVEL

ADJUSTED STRING LINE

LEVEL MARK

3 Digging the trench. Starting at the lowest grade point, dig a trench 1 foot wide along the line that marks the outer edge of the wall. Measure frequently from the line that marks the top of the wall down to the trench bottom to be sure that the trench is level; for a wall 3 feet high, the trench bottom must always be 42 inches below the string line. Remove the stakes.

With a chain saw, cut timbers to fit in the trench, making no timber less than 6 feet long.

Lay out deadman trenches at the wall corners and every 6 feet along its length. For each trench, place the shorter blade of a carpenter's square parallel with an upper edge of the timber, stretch an 8-foot line back from the timber and up the hill parallel to the other blade, and drive a stake into the hill at the end of the line.

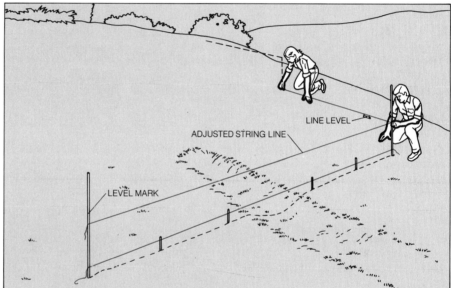

Building the Wall

1 Setting the tilt. Level the first course of timbers in the trench and tilt each timber ¼ inch toward the hill, propping it with small stones. Check the tilt with a ruler and a torpedo level held horizontally across each section; the gap between the bottom of the level and the top of the timber should measure ¼ inch.

At the center of each timber and 6 to 12 inches from each end, drill vertical ⅜-inch holes completely through the timber, using a heavy-duty drill fitted with an electrician's ship-auger bit.

2 Securing the first two courses. Using a 10-pound sledgehammer, drive ⅜-inch steel spikes 42 inches long through the drilled holes in the timbers and into the ground. Check the level of the course and adjust the tilt if necessary. Then lay a second course of timbers upon the first, ¼ inch closer to the hillside. Leave 1-inch gaps between the sections of this course, and stagger the timbers so that the gaps do not align with the joints of the first course. Drill ⅜-inch holes through the timbers and drive ⅜-inch spikes 1 foot long through the holes to pin the layers together.

From the top of the second course dig trenches 6 inches deep, 8 inches wide, and 8 feet long along the routes you have marked for the deadmen; the deadmen themselves will rest upon the second course of timbers. For the crossplates, dig trenches 1 foot deep and 3 feet long across the ends of the deadman trenches.

3 **Bracing the wall.** Cut and lay the deadmen and crossplates. Drive 42-inch steel spikes down through the deadmen and crossplates and into the ground, and drive 12-inch spikes through the deadmen and into the second course.

To start the third course of the wall, cut squared timbers to fit between the ends of the deadmen. Set the first timber next to a corner deadman and spike it in place.

4 **Cutting tight joints.** Set a second timber next to the first, butting the ends together, and make a cut across the butted ends with a chain saw; clean away the wood chips and push the timbers together. Drill a hole diagonally through the top of one timber, across the joint, down through the adjacent timber and into the second course of timbers below; drive a 12-inch spike through this hole to pin all three timbers together. Repeat this procedure until you have completed the third course.

Dos and Don'ts for Chain Saws

A gas-powered chain saw has a chain of sharp teeth that rotate around a 16- to 20-inch guide bar. An automatic or manual oiler lubricates both chain and guide bar to keep them from overheating during operation. A well-made saw can cut heavy timbers in seconds.

Chain saws must be carefully maintained and operated. When you rent one, be sure that the teeth are sharp and the chain is tight—you should never be able to pull the chain more than ⅛ inch away from the bar. Check that the saw has a safety bar and that you have enough fuel and lubricating oil for your job. Have the dealer demonstrate starting and stopping procedures and watch him cut some scrap wood. When you use the saw, follow these rules:
☐ Before cutting a timber, remove all debris from the work area, remove any nails from the wood, and make sure that the timber is well supported. With a combination square, mark guidelines on the timbers you plan to cut.
☐ When you start the saw, rest its body on the ground, steadying it by putting your foot on the brace built into the back handle on most chain saws.
☐ Use two hands to raise the saw.
☐ Make sure no one is near you when you work. Caution: a chain saw makes a deafening noise (you may want to shield your ears); always make sure that no one is behind you before you remove the saw from its cutting position.
☐ While you cut a timber, brace the saw by pushing the prongs next to the blade into the wood.

5 **Laying a drainage run.** Shovel a bed of gravel 12 inches wide and 6 inches deep along the back of the wall, and run a length of 4-inch perforated drain tile along the top of the bed. At the back of the wall, nail a length of galvanized screening over the drainage gaps in the second course of timbers, then cover both the drain tile and the screening with a 6-inch layer of gravel.

6 **Interlocking the corners.** After completing the fourth course of timbers and spiking it to the corner deadmen, lay in the side-wall timbers and secure them with 12-inch spikes. Lay in the fifth course of timbers for the front wall and spike it in place. Then drill holes through the side-wall timbers: one vertically into the end of the fourth course, another horizontally into the fifth course. Drive 12-inch spikes through these holes to secure the corners. Using the same method, and alternating front and side-wall timbers at the ends, build the remaining side-wall and retaining courses; be sure to stagger the timber joints and to set each course ¼ inch closer to the hillside than the one below.

Spread a 4-inch layer of backfill behind the wall and tamp it with a hand- or gas-powered tamper. Spread and tamp additional 4-inch layers until the fill is level with the top of the wall, then add a final layer of topping soil or gravel, sloped slightly up the hill for drainage.

Easy-to-Build Barriers of Vertical Posts

For a simple retaining wall up to 18 inches high, plant a row of vertical timbers in the ground and spike the timbers together with bars of reinforcing steel. The wall is not as strong as a horizontal wall with deadmen, but it is easier to build and useful for such small projects as tree wells and raised planting beds.

The top of the wall need not be level—timbers of different heights make an attractive effect—and you can, if you like, use "found" materials such as old pier pilings, telephone poles or even logs stripped of their bark. Make the basic trench for the timbers as deep as the wall is high, but at the corner posts and at every fifth timber, use a posthole digger *(right)* to double the depth of the trench. For example, a wall 18 inches high calls for a trench 18 inches deep, but the corner and every fifth timber should be sunk in holes that are 36 inches deep.

Once the trench is dug, you need only insert the timbers one by one, starting at a corner, spike them together, fill the trench with dirt and use a hand tamper to compact the fill.

1 **Digging the trenches.** Lay out the face of the trench with a series of stakes driven every two feet and dig a basic trench to the depth of the wall height; then, straddling the corner of the trench, use a posthole digger to make a hole for a single timber twice the depth of the basic trench. When you have laid and pinned four timbers by the method shown below, use the posthole digger to make another deep hole, and repeat the procedure for every fifth timber.

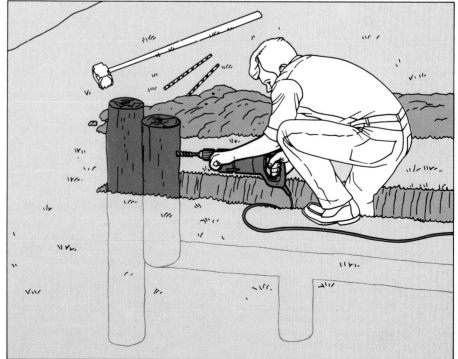

2 **Pinning the wall together.** Set the corner post in its hole, set a post next to it, and drill two horizontal ⅜-inch holes, one above grade and one below, through one timber and into the next. Drive ⅜-inch spikes into the holes. Repeat the procedure on every post, staggering the levels of the drilled holes so that spikes do not collide.

Designing and Building a Free-Form Garden Pool

Few additions lend more charm to a garden than a sunken pool. While prefabricated pools of plastic, fiberglass or metal resist frost damage and are easy to install, they come in a limited variety of shapes and sizes. Working with concrete, you can pick the size, shape and depth that suit you—for a water garden, a fish pond or a wading pool or for a decorative setting for a fountain or waterfall. In areas of moderate frost, the reinforced bowl shape of the pool on the following pages will keep the possibility of frost damage to a minimum, and it is suitable for small to medium sizes, up to about 7,000 gallons' capacity.

Choose a site free of large rocks or tree roots—to make sure, dig a series of test holes about 2½ feet deep with a posthole digger. A level site is easiest to work with, but you may prefer a slight grade—perhaps to provide a gravity drain at the low end of the pool, or to incorporate a

waterfall on the high side. If you do build on a slope, you will have to provide a concrete lip on the downhill side of the pool at the same level as the upper lip, and you may have to grade the ground on the lower side to make the built-up lip less obtrusive.

When you are satisfied with the location, prepare a scale drawing of the pool and take it with you to your building supplier for an estimate of concrete and reinforcing materials you will need. A garden pool requires a fairly stiff mixture of concrete, consisting of 1 part portland cement, 2 parts sand and 3 parts washed stones or small aggregate, plus an additive to aid the formation of tiny air bubbles that make the mix easier to pour and make the finished concrete more resistant to freezing and cracking. To allow for errors, purchase about 10 per cent more of each ingredient than your estimated needs—check with the supplier to

be sure you will be able to return any unopened bags. If your plan calls for more than 1 cubic yard of concrete—the pool shown here requires about 2½ cubic yards of mix—you will need to rent a mixer you can set up at the work area.

You will also need overlapping sections of 10-gauge 6 × 6 wire mesh to line the bottom and sides of the pool, and ⅜-inch steel reinforcing rods, or rebar, to strengthen the concrete lip. Since the rebar should be cut to size on the job, plan on renting a rebar cutter.

On the job itself, you will be handling several tons of earth and concrete; enlist a helper or two before excavating or pouring. Dig a hole that forms an exact bowl-shaped mold for the concrete; the bowl must rest on a base of undisturbed soil, and for that reason you should not refill any part of the hole with dug-out soil: that could cause the concrete to settle unevenly and possibly crack.

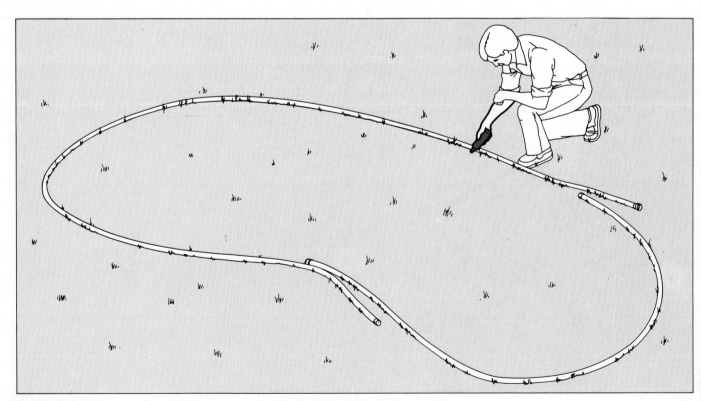

1 **Drawing the pool.** Outline the pool with a rope or length of garden hose and transfer the outline to the ground by squirting chalk dust over the rope or hose from a squeeze bottle. Dig the hole 5 inches larger in every dimension to allow for

the thickness of the concrete, and bevel the sides of the hole to a 45° angle.

For the construction method described here, make the hole no more than 30 inches deep.

2 **Leveling the lip.** Drive 18-inch stakes at 3-foot intervals around the rim of the pool, 6 inches out from the edge; then place one end of a water-level hose *(page 10)* against a stake on the upper slope, with the water in the hose 5 inches above the ground. Have a helper move the other end of the hose around the pool, marking each of the stakes at the same level.

3 **Installing vertical support rods.** Cut ⅜-inch reinforcing rods into 20-inch lengths by inserting the bar into a rented cutter mounted on a 2-by-10 board and, standing on the board, pushing downward on the cutter handle. Pound the rods into the ground halfway between the stakes and the edge of the hole, bringing their tops 2 inches below the level marks on the stakes.

4 **Bending the horizontal rods.** To shape reinforcing rods to the curvature of the pool, slide a length of rigid plumbing pipe over the end of a rod, step on the rod and gradually pull the pipe toward you. As you bend the rods, lay them in position next to the vertical support rods, overlapping adjacent ends by 12 inches. After bending the last rod, trim it to size with the cutter.

5 **Making the frame.** Hold an 8-foot length of the bent reinforcing rod to the tops of three adjoining vertical rods; if the bent rod does not span all three, drive an additional vertical rod near the end of the horizontal one. Secure the bent rods to one another and to the vertical rods with short strips of tie wire *(inset)*.

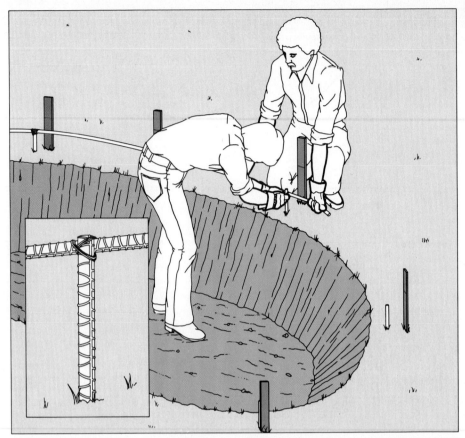

6 **Fitting the mesh.** Bend sheets of 10-gauge 6 × 6 wire reinforcing mesh to cover the bottom and sides of the pool and extend 3 inches beyond the reinforcing-rod rim. Overlap the sheets a few inches, and trim the outer edges with wire cutters to fit them to the shape of the pool. When the pool and its rim are completely covered, lift the mesh one sheet at a time and place bricks on the dirt, flat side up and spaced 1 foot apart. Secure overlaps between sheets with tie wire, then bend the mesh edges over the frame of reinforcing bar and tie them to the frame. To provide a depth gauge for the concrete lining, drive 15-inch pegs cut from reinforcing bar into the bottom and sides of the pool at 2-foot intervals so that they protrude 5 inches.

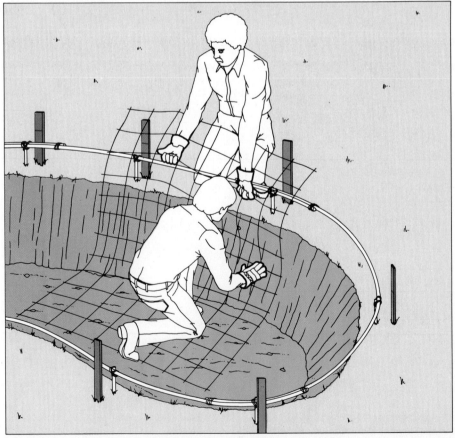

7 **Fitting an overflow pipe.** Join two 1-foot lengths of ¾-inch plastic plumbing pipe to a 90° elbow, and insert one end through the mesh at ground level with the elbow 5 inches inside the mesh at the rim of the pool. Turn the assembly so that the inside end points straight up. To hold the overflow pipe steady while the concrete is poured, wedge it in place with bricks or rocks and secure it to the mesh with tie wire.

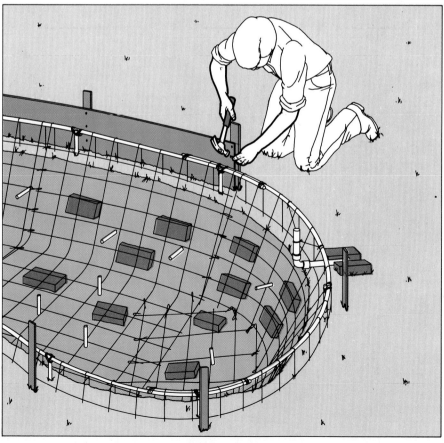

8 **Making the forms.** Cut strips of ⅛-inch hardboard 6 feet long and tapered to meet the level marks on the stakes; nail the strips to the insides of the stakes with their top edges at the level marks on the stakes. Notch the hardboard to fit around the overflow pipe. Brush vegetable oil onto the inner surfaces of the hardboard strips to prevent them from sticking to the concrete.

9 **Pouring the concrete.** To support your wheelbarrow while pouring, prop a platform made of cross-braced 2-by-6 boards and ¾-inch plywood, on cement blocks. Have a helper, standing in the pool on two scraps of plywood, spread the concrete around the bottom and up the sides until the mix is even with the peg tops.

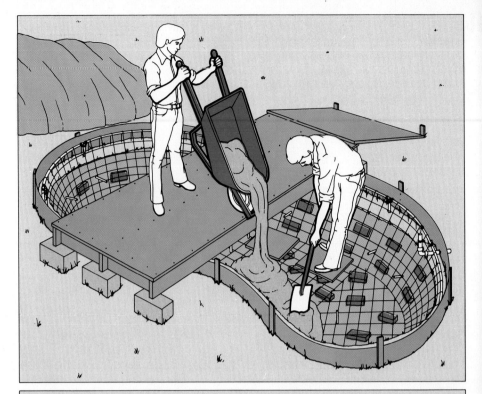

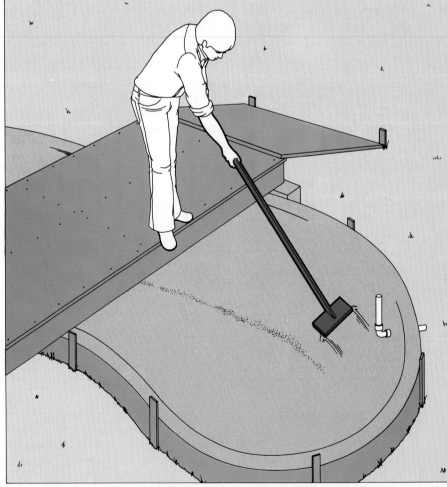

10 **Floating and troweling.** Smooth the concrete with a long-handled wood float made with a 6-foot length of 2-by-2 cut at a 60° angle at one end and nailed to a 1-foot length of 1-by-6 board. Rub the concrete lightly and evenly until all the depth pegs are just below the surface. Shape and smooth the lip with a mason's trowel.

1 **Finishing the surface.** Draw a stiff-bristled broom across the concrete to roughen and ridge the surfaces. If the concrete sets so quickly that the bristles leave little or no impression, spray it lightly with water to soften it temporarily. When the concrete has cured—in about 3 days— coat the surface with waterproof paint or a pool sealer and plug any gaps around the overflow pipe with polyurethane caulking. Saw the top of the overflow pipe off just below the pool rim; cover the pipe intake with a disk of fiberglass screening secured with a plastic hose clamp.

The Finishing Touches

Stores that stock equipment for swimming pools, gardens or aquariums sell a wide variety of materials to help you keep your pool looking distinctively attractive. Among them:

☐ Plastic, vinyl or silicone paints are available in numerous colors—including black, which, to the surprise of some people, is the choice of most landscape designers and offers many advantages. It looks natural and gives an illusion of great depth. And because it absorbs heat, it helps to protect fish and plants from the shock of a sudden frost or from cold weather.

☐ Pools holding more than 500 gallons should be equipped with an electric re-circulating pump to aerate the water and prevent it from becoming stagnant. There are two kinds of pumps: the submersible type, placed in the pool and hidden beneath plants or a stone shelf; and the nonsubmersible type, generally placed in a shallow wellhole next to the pool. Pumps are rated by the number of gallons of water they can circulate in one hour; a unit with a rating of 170 to 300 gallons per hour (referred to as GPH by pump manufacturers) is adequate for most pools.

☐ If you plan to use your pool as a fish pond or a setting for water plants, buy a powdered neutralizing agent from a masonry dealer or garden-supply store. Mixed with water, the powder becomes a sealer that neutralizes the harmful al-kalis in freshly cured concrete. The alka-lis can also be neutralized by filling the pool with a solution of 1 quart of vin-egar to every 100 gallons of water. Leave the solution in the pool for three days, drain it off and scrub the pool with a stiff brush. After rinsing, refill with fresh water and plant water lilies in pots set on the pool bottom, or water hyacinths that float on the surface. Lotus, *Azolla* and *Elodea* also are often used.

☐ Algae growth, a recurrent problem in still pools, can be curbed by such scav-engers as snails, turtles and frogs; an efficient way to control insect pests, such as mosquitoes, that could thrive in the pool's still water is to stock the pool with goldfish.

2

Borders of Wood, Brick and Iron

A fence-building aid. A picket board held base side up makes a simple but ingenious spacer to position a picket for nailing to the upper support of a fence panel. Painting the pickets before they are attached simplifies finishing work. Scratches and hammer marks made during construction can be easily touched up after the fence has been completed.

There are many reasons for fences, and there is a fence for almost every purpose. A tall fence can appropriately surround a swimming pool, an outdoor room, a sun-bathing pocket or an entire yard. Short labyrinthine baffles can block the outside view of a bedroom window or a glass-walled bathroom, or the view through a fence entryway. You can achieve either total privacy with a brick, board or panel fence, or partial privacy with a louvered, grape-stake, picket or board-on-board fence. In addition to providing privacy, fences can enclose areas, fend off the elements, embellish your house and land, or perform all these functions at once. Used as a boundary, a fence says, with emphasis that depends on height and construction, "Don't cross." In a friendly, good-fences-make-good-neighbors way, such a barrier can keep out animals, cyclists and shortcutters, and prevent trespasses that could cause friction between neighbors.

Because property-line fences involve other people, they are subject to zoning or building-code regulations that vary from community to community. Codes may establish height, or the fence's setback from a street to ensure visibility for drivers. In many places a fence built by one neighbor on a property line automatically becomes the joint property of both neighbors. And if you incorrectly locate a fence beyond your property, the mistake is costly to remedy.

Boundary-marking contributes to privacy, but fences also influence the environment—even the climate—around your house. A fence can temper the wind—though, paradoxically, a solid fence makes a poor windbreak; the flow of air over the top creates a tumbling eddy that pulls the wind back to the ground. An open picket, slat, louvered or lattice fence, however, will generally slow the wind and reduce its chilling effect. In some cases, open fences can be angled to funnel summer breezes, increasing their velocity so that the funnel area seems cooler than the rest of the yard. Solid fences that reach the ground dam the flow of frost—a peril to tender plants upstream of the dam but a boon to those below.

To enhance your property's appearance, choose a fence style that avoids either an exact match with the house (a clapboard fence for a clapboard house) or a head-on clash. Consider matching an element of a house (brick pilasters and an iron fence for a classical brick house) or creating a deliberate but tasteful contrast (a grape-stake fence for a colonial house). A plain fence can set off plantings; a handsome fence that hides a garbage can or a compost heap does double duty. Many fences look better from one side than from the other; usually you will want to show the world the more attractive side. Your neighbor will thank you, thus demonstrating once again the accuracy of the old saying about good fences.

Setting Fence Posts Straight and Secure

The key to a good-looking, long-lasting fence is a series of sturdy fence posts, securely anchored and properly aligned and spaced. The posts are the working members of a fence, bearing and bracing the gates and railings. But the posts are also an important element in the design of a fence, creating evenly spaced visual breaks in long runs of railings or panels.

Generally, the function and size of the fence determines the characteristics of its posts. Heavy fences and any fence more than 4 feet high should be supported by posts no smaller than 4-by-4-inch lumber. Low picket fences can be anchored with 2-by-4 intermediate, or line, posts but even on a lightweight fence the end, corner and gateposts should be at least 4-by-4s. Use pressure-treated lumber, impregnated with wood preservative under pressure so that the entire post is resistant to rot and fungus. Pressure-treated posts last up to 20 years, while untreated posts may have to be replaced after five.

The depth of the posthole and what filling to use within it are the next considerations. As a general rule, one third of the post should be belowground; a 6-foot fence, for example, requires 9-foot posts sunk 3 feet into the earth. In relatively stable soil, tamped earth or gravel will hold the post securely. Concrete

makes a more secure setting and is advisable in loose or sandy soils. The gateposts and the end and corner posts, which are subjected to greater stress, should be set in concrete wherever possible; if you prefer not to go to the trouble and expense of using concrete, use longer lengths of lumber for these key posts and sink them deeper into the ground.

Though concrete settings provide the most solid base, they are subject to frost damage in colder climates. As freezing water expands under and around the setting, a phenomenon known as frost heaving tends to force the post up out of the ground. If the frost depth in your area is quite shallow, you can set the concrete below the frost line, but it is generally impractical to sink posts deeper than 3 to 3½ feet. To minimize frost heaving in shallower postholes, widen the hole at the base into a bell shape so that the surrounding earth holds the concrete in place. If wet posts in your locality sometimes freeze and expand, and crack concrete footings, drive wood shims between the post and the concrete while the concrete is still wet. Then remove the shims and fill the gaps with roofing cement after the concrete has set.

The exposed end grain at each end of the post requires additional protection.

To prevent the bottom from resting in ground water, shovel several inches of gravel into each hole to act as a drain. To help protect the top from rain, cut the post at a 30° to 45° angle, or cover it with a metal post cap, available at hardware stores to fit standard post sizes.

Post spacings are determined by the standardized widths of fence sections and railings; and if you build your own fence, it is simpler to use standard lumber sizes to reduce cutting and fitting on the job. In general, posts should not be spaced more than 8 feet apart; at this spacing, a standard 16-foot length of lumber spans three posts. After measuring the length of the fence and allowing for gates, you may find that you must use tighter spacing and shorter lengths of lumber to avoid ending a fence with a noticeably narrow section.

Measuring and marking post locations is relatively simple on flat ground; on sloping or uneven ground the type of fence determines the measuring method. For fences that slope, measurements should be made along the surface. For fences of panels with level tops, measure spacings along a level line above the ground. On hillsides, the panels are often stepped down in level sections, with posts evenly spaced along a level line.

Where to Place Postholes

Locating posts on flat ground. Drive stakes at the locations of the end posts, stretch a string between the stakes, just high enough to clear the ground, and measure the length of the string to determine the standard lengths of lumber or fencing that will make up the fence with a minimum of cutting. Make a gauge pole—a piece of straight 1-by-2 lumber cut to the length of the fence sections and marked off in 1-foot increments—and set it repeatedly on the ground against the string to set the locations of the intermediate posts. Use the markings on the pole to adjust locations for gateposts and to avoid ending the fence with a very short section.

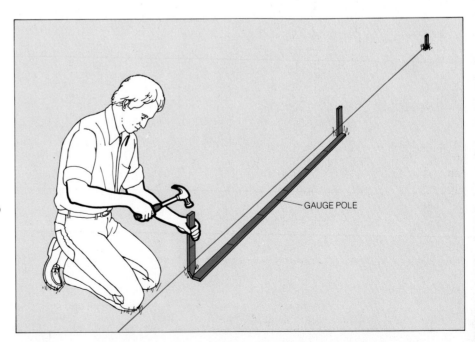

GAUGE POLE

Staking posts on uneven ground. For a fence with rigid rectangular panels, or one with a level top, such as a picket fence *(page 43)*, stretch a line between two end stakes, level it with a line level and, working with a helper if necessary, measure along it with a gauge pole. Drop a plumb bob from the line to pinpoint each post location on the ground *(below, top)* and drive marker stakes at all the post locations. For a fence such as a post-and-rail *(page 49)*, with a top that follows the natural contours of the ground, drive stakes at the fence ends and at each high and low point in between. Join all the stakes with string and use a gauge pole to space the remaining posts evenly between the post locations already marked *(below, bottom)*.

To run a straight line of string over hills or in areas with heavy undergrowth or other obstructions, use the sighting techniques on page 13.

Using a posthole digger. After removing the marker stake, use a manual posthole digger or hand auger to dig a posthole. For a post set in concrete, make the hole at least three times the post width and angle the digger to widen the bottom. For posts set in tamped earth, dig a hole that is twice the post width. Make the hole about 6 inches deeper than the depth of the post belowground. Fill the bottom with 4 to 6 inches of gravel, topped with a flat rock.

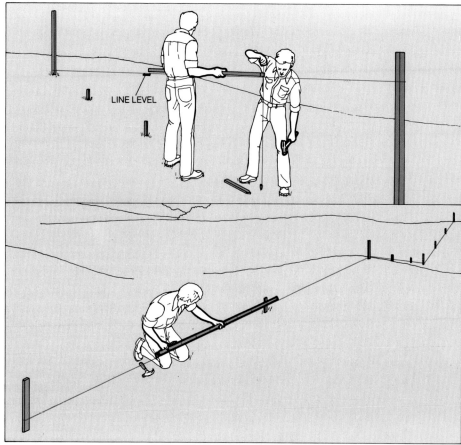

LINE LEVEL

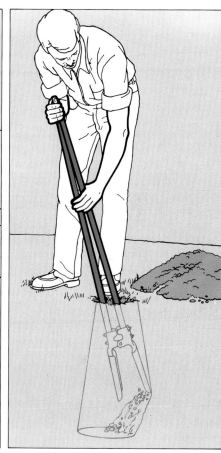

A Timesaving Tool for Digging Holes

A gasoline-powered auger, available from tool-rental shops, saves both time and effort, especially if you are setting 10 or more fence posts, unless you are working in very rocky soil.

Power augers weigh between 35 and 40 pounds and come with a removable spiral-shaped boring bit that can excavate holes up to 4 feet deep. Some models can be operated by one person, but the two-man auger at right is safer to use, because the bit is braced by handles on two sides and is less likely to kick out of the hole when it hits a rock or other obstruction.

To use a power auger, mark the depth of the posthole on the bit with tape and set it over the marked position. Turn on the motor, adjust the speed with the handle-mounted clutch and exert an even downward pressure from both sides. After digging a few inches, slowly raise the bit to clear the dirt from the hole. If you hit a rock, stop the motor and use a digging bar or pick and shovel to pry it loose.

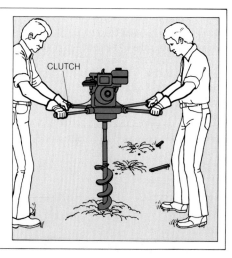

CLUTCH

Getting Your Posts in Line

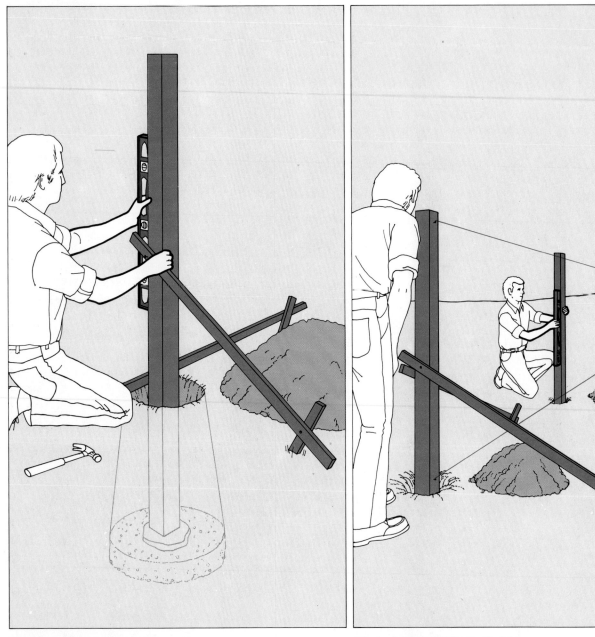

Bracing an end post plumb. Drive two stakes on adjacent sides of the posthole and fasten a 1-by-2-inch bracing board to each stake with a single nail. Set an end post in the hole, centered over the flat stone at the bottom, and use a carpenter's level to plumb a side of the post adjacent to a bracing board. When that side is plumb, nail the upper end of the bracing board to the post. Then plumb the side adjacent to the other board and nail that board to the post. Brace the other end post in the same way.

Aligning intermediate posts. Stretch two strings between the sides of the end posts, one near the top and the other close to ground level. While a helper aligns one side of an intermediate post with the two strings and plumbs an adjacent side with a level, sight along the top string to check both the post height and the alignment. To make minor adjustments in height, add or remove gravel; to alter alignment, move the rock on which the post is centered.

If the posts are anchored in tamped earth, fill the holes with soil or gravel and tamp (*opposite*) as you set each post; if you are setting the posts in concrete, brace all the posts as shown until the concrete has hardened (*above, left*).

Two Ways to a Secure Support

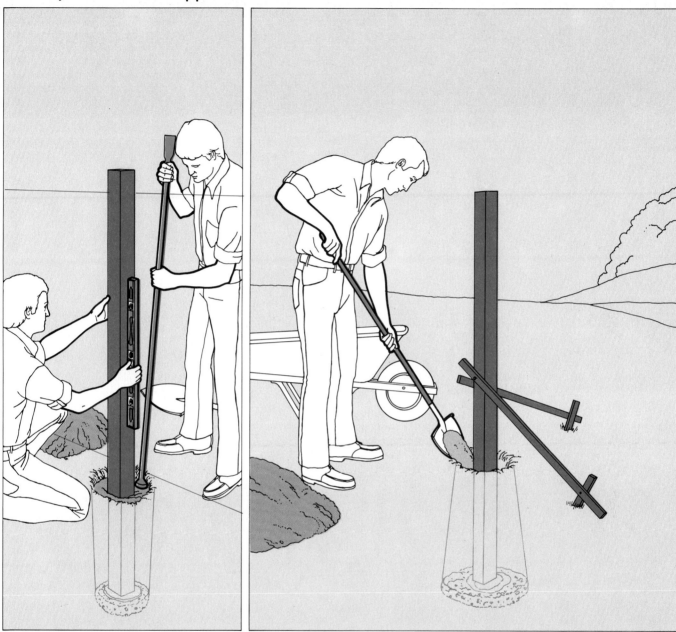

In tamped earth. While a helper holds the posts plumb, fill the hole with earth, in 3- to 4-inch layers; as each layer is put in, tamp the soil with the flat end of a digging bar (*above*) or a 2-by-4. Overfill the hole and shape a cone of earth around the post to channel away runoff.

In concrete. Check the braced post for alignment and plumb, then fill the hole with a thin concrete mix—one part cement, three parts sand and five parts gravel. Overfill the hole slightly and use a trowel to bevel the concrete down from the post for runoff. Within 20 minutes, recheck the post for plumb and make small adjustments, adding additional concrete as necessary. Allow the concrete to set for at least 24 hours before removing the braces or attaching fencing. If the concrete leaves a slight gap around the posts as it dries, caulk the space or fill it with roofing cement.

To save both concrete and the effort of mixing it, some professionals simply empty half a bag of dry premixed concrete into the hole on top of the gravel and fill the rest of the hole with earth. Though this is not as strong as a full concrete setting, natural seepage of ground water will eventually solidify the concrete base while the tamped earth holds the post up.

Repairing and Replacing Posts

The best-anchored posts will eventually succumb to frost, rot, wind or general wear and tear. To repair the damage, you must either realign a sound post or replace—wholly or in part—any post that is split or rotted.

Posts forced slightly out of alignment by wind or frost can often be pushed back into position and secured by re-tamping the earth around them or by driving wood shims between a post and its concrete base. A steeply leaning post may need to be braced by a length of steel pipe or reinforcing rod.

Damage to the upper half of a post can be repaired with a new section spliced to the base (*opposite*). If the base is unsound, replace the entire post. Sometimes the location of a post can be moved a foot or two without extensive cutting of fence rails or panels; in this situation, simply set a new post in the new location and saw off the old one flush with the ground. Otherwise, you must drill and chisel out the rotted stump or, if necessary, uncover the entire setting, then break up the concrete into manageable chunks with a crowbar or digging bar and pour a new setting.

Fixing a sagging post. If wood wedges around the base do not hold a post vertical, use steel pipe and a heavy-gauge perforated metal strap to pull the post into alignment. On the side away from the sag, drive a 5- to 6-foot length of 1½-inch pipe halfway into the ground just clear of the concrete footing. Nail one end of the strap to one side of the post, loop the strap around the top of the pipe and, while a helper pushes the post back to plumb, nail the other end of the strap to the opposite side of the post.

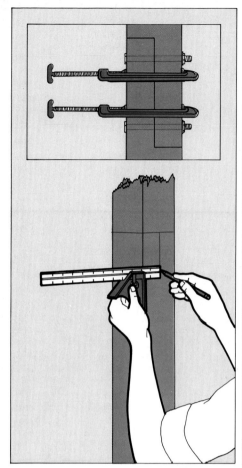

Replacing the top of a post. Use a combination square to mark a cutting line around the post below the damaged part and to draw an 8-inch vertical mark down the center of one side of the post; from the bottom of the vertical mark, extend a horizontal mark to the post edge. Duplicate the marks on the opposite side of the post, cut off the damaged section and saw out the wood inside the marks for a lap joint. Cut a matching joint on the new post section and glue and clamp the joint. When the glue has set but before you remove the clamps, drill two bolt holes through the lapped sections (*inset*) and secure the joint with 4-inch galvanized bolts.

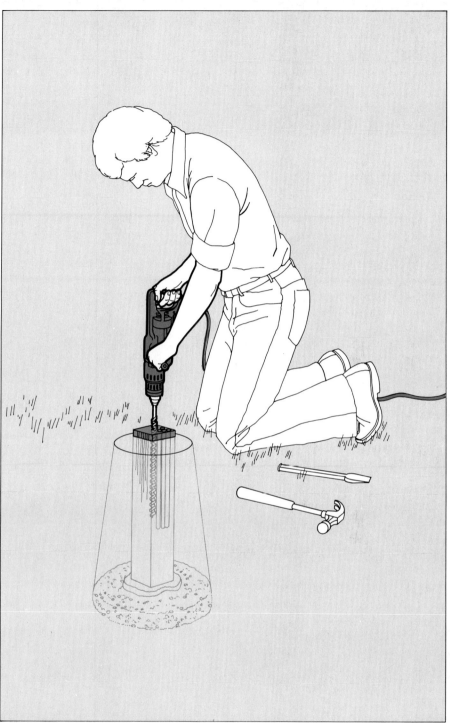

Replacing a post. Saw the post off a few inches above its concrete setting and drill a number of holes down into the center of the stump using an electrician's bit 18 inches long in a heavy-duty, ½-inch drill. Keep the drill bit clear of the concrete. Use a cold chisel or pry bar to split and loosen the stump, and when all the wood is out, set the new post in the hole. If the post is too small, drive shims around the base while a helper plumbs the post; if it is too wide, taper the end with a hammer and chisel.

Wooden Fences: Variations on a Basic Theme

Almost every wooden fence is built on a framework of upright posts and connecting rails, or stringers. This simple skeleton can carry a range of fences that will meet practically any need. A fence of nothing more than posts and rails makes a clear boundary marker, adapts well to rough or rolling terrain and covers the most ground with the least lumber. Siding nailed to a post-and-stringer frame can take the shape of a low picket fence to decorate the border of a front yard or a tall board fence to insure privacy or keep children and pets within bounds.

In all of these fence styles, your first concern is the quality of the building materials. Use pressure-treated lumber or naturally decay- and insect-resistant woods, such as cedar or redwood. All are more expensive than construction-grade lumber, but they will last longer.

If you cannot get pressure-treated lumber in the sizes you want, treat the wood yourself. Soak board ends in pentachlorophenol or copper naphthenate. The latter will stain the wood light green but, unlike some other preservatives, it will not harm garden plants. If you cannot soak the lumber, paint it liberally with preservative, using especially heavy coats at sawn ends. While you assemble the fence, daub additional coats of preservative on fresh cuts and adjoining surfaces. If you intend to paint the fence, paint all of the lumber before beginning to assemble it. Use stainless-steel, hot-dipped galvanized, or aluminum fasteners, which will not rust and stain the fence.

The basic post-and-board fence on these pages is made of 1-inch lumber, face-nailed to 4-by-4 posts. The posts—36 to 42 inches high for a three-rail fence,

48 to 54 inches for a four-rail one—can be topped with metal post caps or with an angled cap rail (right) to protect the ends, which rot easily, from moisture. Space the posts to use standard lengths of board lumber as much as possible.

Post-and-rail fences, with tapered rail ends that fit into mortised posts, are sturdier than post-and-board fences and almost as easy to install. Prefabricated mortised posts and tapered stringers are sold by lumber suppliers in a variety of styles. All are assembled like the split-rail fence illustrated on page 42.

Picket fences can also be built in a wide range of styles, though prefabricated pickets are becoming difficult to find in some areas. A picket fence can be any desired height but is usually 3 to 4 feet, with pickets projecting about 6 inches above the top stringer.

The Simplest Fence of All

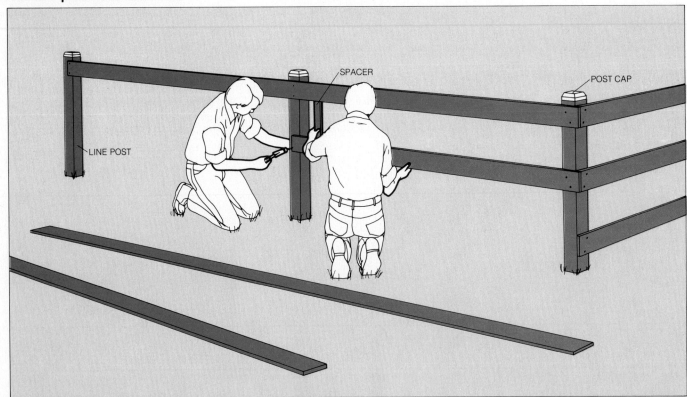

SPACER

POST CAP

LINE POST

Building a post-and-board fence. To start from an end or corner, trim 1-by-4 or 1-by-6 boards to extend from a corner or end post to the center of the second line post, and stagger these long boards with others extending only to the center of the first line post. Nail on these boards. Use a piece of scrap wood as a spacer to position the lower rails. Continue to add boards cut to the longer length until you need short pieces for ends. Nail metal caps onto the posts.

Desirable Extras: A Cap Rail and Battens

1 Beveling the posts. To prepare the posts for the cap, saw a 30° angle at their ends—you can start the cut with a power saw set to the angle, but it will not cut all the way through and you must finish with a handsaw. To prepare a corner post, make a second cut at a 30° angle across an adjacent side (*below, right*).

Set all posts, placing the corner ones so that their bevels slant to support mitered cap rails.

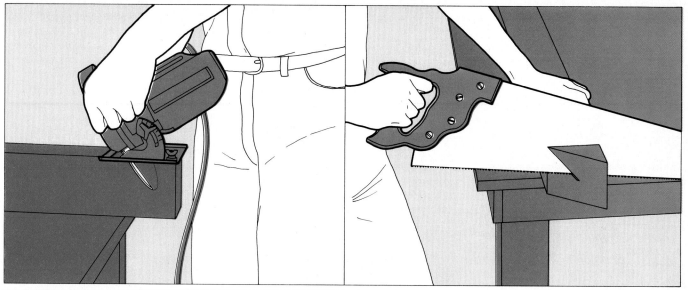

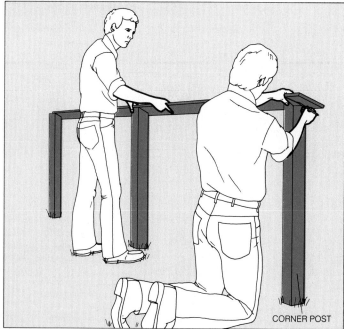

CORNER POST

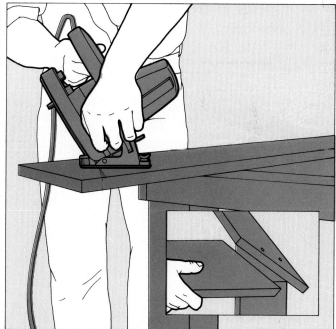

2 Marking the cap rail. With a helper, hold a 1-by-6 in position on top of a corner post and a line post. Have the helper set one end of the board at the center of the line post while you mark the underside of the board along the angle of the corner-post top. Then mark a second 1-by-6 cap-rail board to fit across the other angled face of the corner post. Use a carpenter's square to transfer the marks to the other side of each board to facilitate sawing.

3 Cutting the cap rail. With a circular saw, cut the rails along the corner-post marks at 30°, beveling the ends of the boards so that they can be mitered flush.

Nail the cap-rail sections to the corner and line posts, aligning the tops of the rails with the top edges of the beveled posts (*inset*).

4 **Installing the battens.** When all the rails are fastened, cut 1-inch-thick batten boards to reach from the underside of the cap rail to an inch or two off the ground and nail them to the posts.

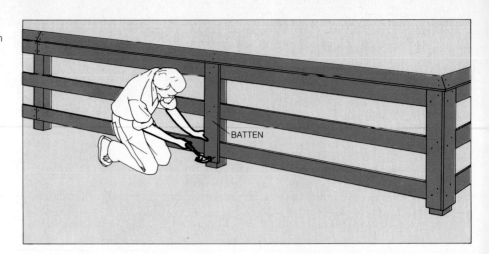

BATTEN

Fitting Together a Rail Fence

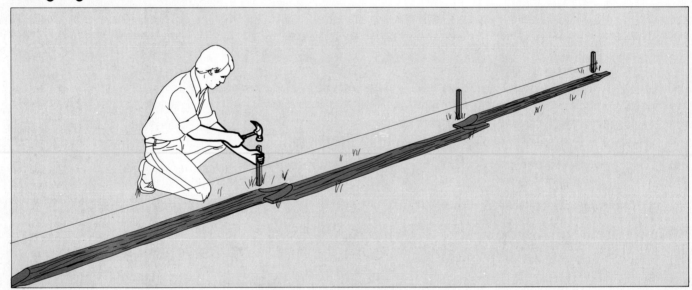

1 **A dry run of rails.** Drive stakes for the end posts and string a line between them (*page 34*). Lay precut rails on the ground along the fence line, overlapped as they will be in the mortises of the posts—if the rails do not fit evenly, move the end stakes if possible or cut short rails for one or two sections of the fence. Drive additional stakes at the centers of the overlaps. Dig holes for the posts at the stake locations.

2 **Fitting the rails in place.** Set an end post in tamped earth (*page 37*) and lower the first line post into its hole; then insert the ends of the rails into the slots of the end post and, as you lift the line post upright, fit the other ends of the rails into the line-post mortises. Plumb the line post, secure it with tamped earth and set succeeding sections the same way.

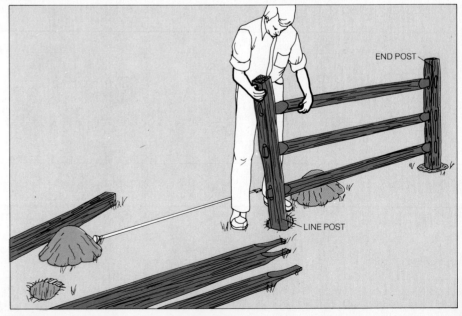

END POST

LINE POST

Putting Up a Picket Fence

1 **Installing the stringers.** For the bottom stringers, trim 2-by-4s to fit between each pair of posts and nail galvanized 4-inch angle irons to their ends. Attach the stringers to the posts about 8 inches above the ground, nailing through the angle irons and then toenailing.

Use long 2-by-4s for top stringers to span as many posts as possible. Nail them on top of the posts, cutting them to meet in the centers of line and corner posts. At line posts, bevel the stringer ends at an angle of 45° so that they overlap; at corner posts, miter the stringer ends.

2 **Attaching the pickets.** Using a piece of scrap the length of a picket, make a spacer as wide as the distance between pickets. Nail a block of wood about 6 inches from one end of the spacer as a cleat; hang the spacer on the fence by hooking the cleat over a top stringer. Set the first picket at the edge of an end post, align its point with the top of the spacer, plumb it with a level and nail it in place. Proceed along the fence, using the spacer to locate each picket. Check with a level every few pickets to be sure they are not drifting out of plumb. Stop a few feet from the end of the fence and check the fit of the remaining pickets; adjust the spacing if necessary, so that the last picket will be flush with the outside edge of the end post.

ANGLE IRON

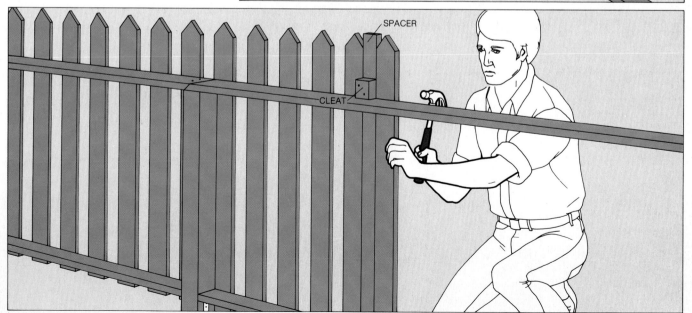

SPACER

CLEAT

Pickets in Patterns

1 Building a panel. Build rectangular frames of 2-by-3s to fit between each pair of posts. Cut picket slats to the length of the longest picket in your pattern and, starting from the ends, nail several of them to the frame laid out on the ground. Align the pickets evenly along the bottom of the frame, using a spacer with a cleat that holds the spacer's end about 4 inches below the frame bottom. In the center of the panel, lay the pickets on the frame without nailing, adjust their spacing, mark their positions on the stringers and nail them in place.

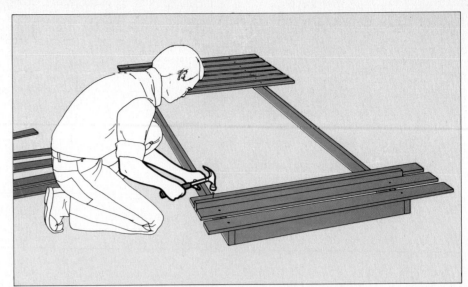

2 Marking a curved pattern. Measure down from the top center of the panel of pickets the full depth of the curve and drive a central nail. Drive two end nails at the top of the picket panel, each a distance from the central nail equal to half the panel length. Tie a cord to one end nail, pull it around the central nail and fasten it to the other end nail. Now remove the central nail, substituting for it the point of a pencil. Keeping the cord taut, use the pencil to draw a curve on the picket panel. Mark each panel in the same manner and cut along the curves.

3 Installing the panels. Have a helper hold each panel in position against the posts so that the post tops fit into the picket pattern. The bottom stringer should be about 8 inches above the ground. Nail the panels to the posts through the uprights and, for additional support, toenail through the bottom stringer from the side.

A Rack of Dowels

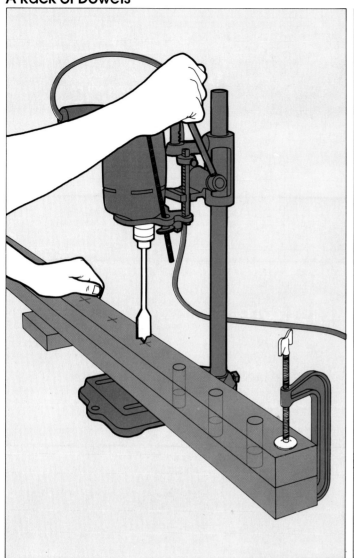

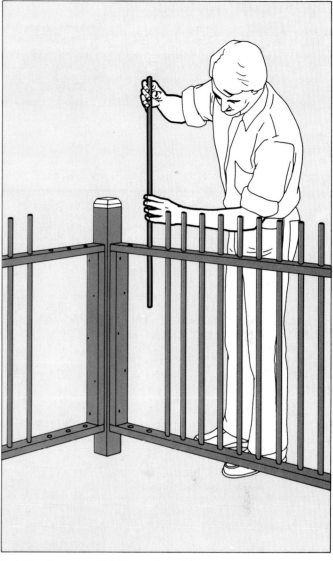

1 Preparing the stringers. Cut 2-by-3 stringers to fit between posts, clamp each pair together and mark the positions for the dowels. Bore ¾-inch holes through the top stringer and a third of the way into the bottom one at each marked point. The holes must be straight; use a drill-press stand or a jig made for guiding dowel holes.

2 Installing the panels. Build frames for a picket panel from the stringer pairs. In all but the last three or four holes at the ends of each panel, insert ¾-inch dowels through the top stringer, resting them in the depressions in the bottom stringer, and glue the dowels to the bottom stringer with exterior-grade carpenter's glue. Finally, nail the fence panels to the posts, and insert and glue the remaining dowels.

Tall Fences for Privacy

Although they are higher and heavier, most privacy fences are built much like the picket fences on page 43. Common lumber nailed to simple post-and-stringer frames will produce a variety of attractive fences; prefabricated panels—in styles ranging from patterned plywood to latticework—can be nailed directly to posts or framed inside posts and stringers.

Some fences, however, require more sophisticated carpentry. A tall louvered fence, for example, is heavier and more prone to warp than some of the simpler designs and should be made with sturdier joints. To build the louvered fence on pages 47-48, you will need a router to cut grooves in the posts and the stringers. The key to using the router safely and effectively is a solidly made jig to guide the bit. Always clamp or nail the jig to whatever you are cutting and make sure the lumber is steady. Wear goggles and keep the router at chest height or below. To make the high cuts in the posts, stand on a stepladder steadied by a helper.

Five Screens for Your Yard

High fences on basic frames. All of the fences at right are supported on frames of 4-by-4 posts and 2-by-4 stringers. The posts are 6 to 8 feet high, set 6 to 8 feet apart. The simplest privacy fence is made of vertical boards or tall narrow slats, like redwood grape stakes, nailed directly to the top and bottom stringers (and to a middle stringer if the fence is taller than 6 feet). Almost as simple is a fence of horizontal boards face-nailed to the posts and to 2-by-4 studs that are toenailed to the top and bottom stringers 24 to 36 inches apart. The same framework will also support solid plywood panels.

A board-and-board fence admits breezes and looks good from either side. Vertical boards are nailed to both sides of the frame, separated by less than their own widths. The boards on one side are positioned opposite the spaces on the other. Ready-made panels in elaborate styles like latticework are mounted against 1-by-2s nailed in advance to the posts and stringers. Instructions for building a latticework panel are on page 93. Ready-made panels or precut boards and vertically grooved posts (*right*) are available for basket-weave fences.

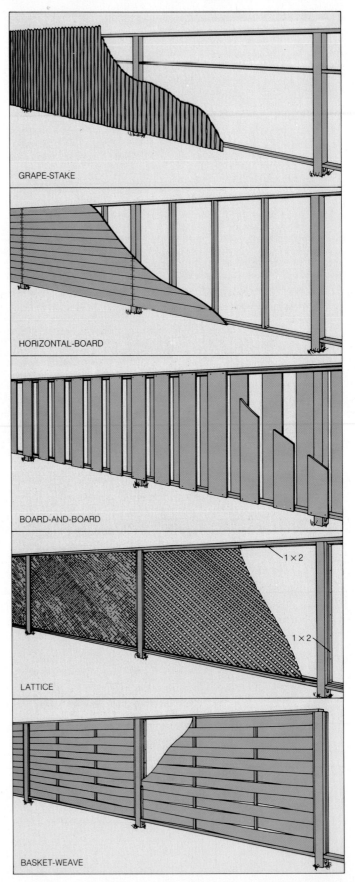

GRAPE-STAKE

HORIZONTAL-BOARD

BOARD-AND-BOARD

1 × 2

1 × 2

LATTICE

BASKET-WEAVE

A Special Frame for Louvers

1 Marking a stringer. Cut two 2-by-4s 1½ inches longer than the distance between two posts. Draw perpendicular lines across both 2-by-4s, ¾ inch in from each end. Stand a scrap 1-by-6 diagonally across one 2-by-4 at the angle you have chosen for the louvers so that one corner touches the pencil line; trace around the 1-by-6. Determine the louver spacing that will produce a good overlap (usually 3 to 4 inches) and mark the intervals on one edge of the 2-by-4, starting from the initial pencil line (*inset*).

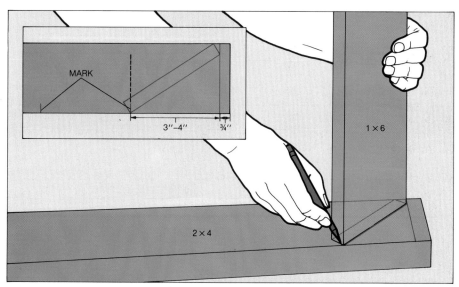

2 Cutting grooves with a router and jig. To make a jig, use a T bevel to transfer the angle traced on the 2-by-4 stringer to a piece of scrap lumber about 2 feet long. Place two short boards on the marked scrap board at this angle, parallel to each other and separated by the diameter of the router base plate; screw them in place. Fit the router with a straight ¾-inch jointing bit, set it to cut a groove ½ inch deep, and cut a 1-inch notch in the crosspiece of the jig by running the router between the two guide boards (*right, top*). Clamp the marked 2-by-4 stringer to a bench and tack the jig to it, aligning the notch in the jig with one of the marks on the stringer (*right, bottom*). Move the router steadily across the 2-by-4; repeat at each mark.

Use the grooved stringer as a template to mark the positions of louvers on the second 2-by-4, and cut grooves in it. Partially assemble the louver panel by slipping two or three 1-by-6 boards into position in the grooves at each end of the stringers and two in the middle; secure them in place by nailing through the stringers.

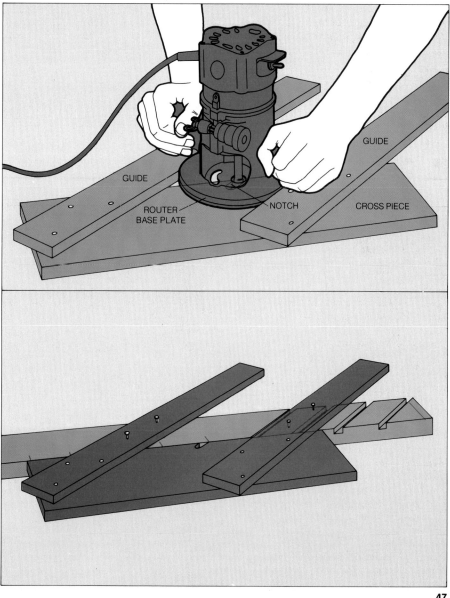

3 **Cutting dados in the posts.** Much as you cut grooves in the stringers, you will use a jig and router to dado the posts. First mark the positions for the lower edges of the top and bottom stringers on each pair of posts. A water level (page 10) will ensure that the marks are perfectly level. Construct a two-guide jig similar to the one in Step 2 but with two crosspieces. Attach the guides at right angles to the crosspieces and ¾ inch farther apart than the diameter of the router base plate. With the same router bit used in Step 2 reset to cut ¾ inch deep, cut a notch in one of the crosspieces by running the router along one guide and then back along the other.

At each mark on the posts, clamp the jig to the post, aligning the notch with the mark. Move the router across the post, running it along the lower guide until it hits the notch, then back along the upper guide to make a 1½-inch dado.

4 **Assembling the fence.** Supporting the bottom stringer on blocks, lift the partially assembled louvered panel upright between the posts, slip the stringers into the dados and toenail them to the posts. Slip the remaining louvers into their grooves, securing them with nails at the top and exterior-grade carpenter's glue at the bottom.

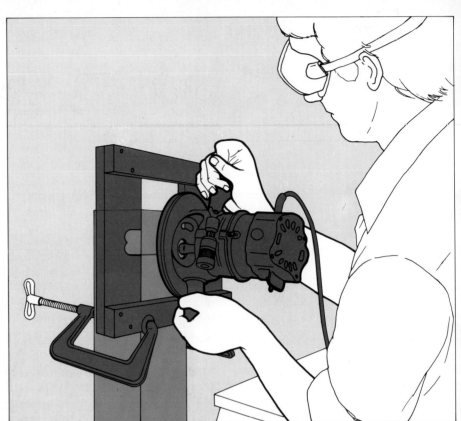

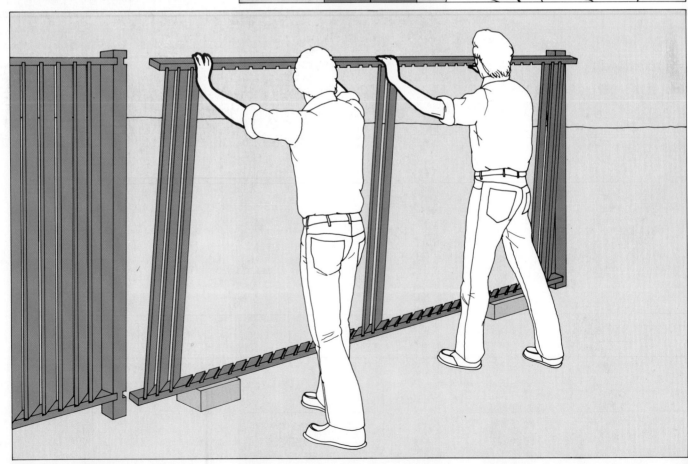

Adapting to Uneven Ground

Building a fence that successfully follows your property's contours often depends on choosing the right style of fence for your land and modifying the design as necessary. A post-and-rail or post-and-board fence *(below)* conforms to any terrain and is best for sharply sloping or rolling ground; a fence with vertical members face-nailed to a post-and-board frame follows the ground almost as well.

On rough but relatively level ground, a fence with vertical pickets or slats *(bottom)* can smooth out small dips and rises; its bottom follows the earth's contours while the top remains level. If you plan to build such a fence, buy enough pickets of extra length to fill in the low spots.

Rectangular-paneled fences are not suited to extremely rough or rolling ground, but they adapt well to steady slopes if built in steps *(page 50)*. Uniform stepping requires a few calculations, but once the posts are in position, attaching stringers and siding is straightforward.

Going up and down hills. Set posts on each rise and in each depression and space the remaining posts between them *(page 35)*. For a post-and-board fence like the one at left, hold or tack the boards in position against the posts and use a level to make vertical marks on the boards at the post centers wherever two boards meet. Trim the boards at the marked angles. If you attach slats or pickets to the stringers, use a spacer *(page 43, Step 2)* to align them evenly at a uniform distance above the top stringer and use a level to plumb them.

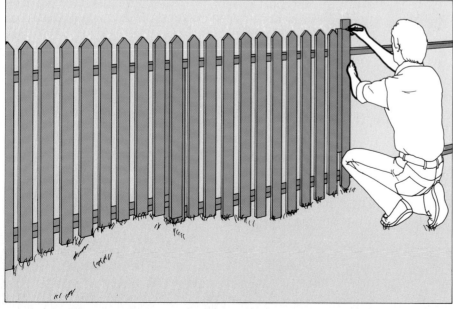

Leveling bumps and dips. To line up pickets on uneven ground, hold each one upside down against the stringers with its shaped top just off the ground. Mark its bottom end even with the top of the spacer you are using to align all the pickets, and trim at the mark.

Stepping down a slope. Run a string from ground level at the top of the slope to a tall stake at the bottom and level it with a line or a water level *(page 35)*. The height of the string on the tall stake is the vertical drop of the hill. For a long or very steep hill, carry out the procedure by installments and total the measurements.

By the method using a string and plumb bob *(described on page 35)*, drive stakes to mark post locations. Divide the number of fence sections into the total vertical drop to calculate the "stringer drop" from one section to the next. Set the top end post to the intended fence height, the rest of the posts to the fence height plus the stringer drop. Starting from the bottom of the hill, attach a top stringer to each post, level it and attach it to the adjacent taller post. Then finish the fence as you would a level one.

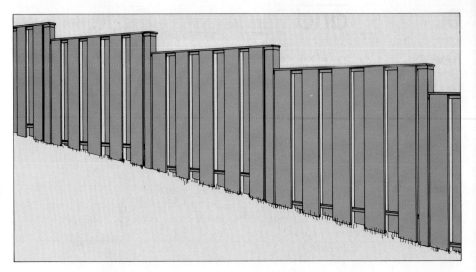

America's First Fences

A familiar maxim of colonial America cautioned farmers to build their fences "horse-high, bull-proof and pig-tight." Most new settlers had few tools and little time for careful carpentry to meet the requirements of this rustic building code; instead, they combined ingenuity with an abundance of materials—most notably in zigzag rail fences like the one in the 1858 print at right.

These early fences were by-products of clearing the land. The settlers heaped into rude barriers the rocks and trees they hauled out of their fields. Their continent's seemingly inexhaustible virgin forests afforded more fencing material than any of them would ever need, and pioneer farmers used it freely.

The Virginia rail, or worm, fence was among the sturdiest and most extravagant of these simple enclosures. It was made of 11- to 12-foot logs stacked one on top of another in a zigzag pattern with their ends interwoven like the fingers of clasped hands. A typical example might stand 10 rails high, angled back and forth across a bed 5 or 6 feet wide and braced where the rails interlocked by pairs of leaning posts crossed over the tops of the rails. The zigzag, or "worm," of the fence gave it stability against "any wind that will not prostrate crops and fruit trees," according to a 19th Century fencing manual. Its top course of rails was the heaviest, to weigh down the rest; slimmer logs in the bottom courses minimized the gaps.

A tall zigzag fence might use nearly 8,000 logs in a mile, and even a modest four- to six-rail fence consumed 20 acres of trees to enclose a 200-acre farm. In lumber-poor Europe, where hedges and ditches separated fields, the American "mania for enclosure" seemed wasteful and bellicose. "The stripping of forests to build fortifications around personal property," editorialized a London newspaper in 1780, "is a perfect example of the way those people in the New World live and think."

Americans could shrug off European criticism, but soon they could not ignore the increasing scarcity of land and lumber in their bountiful New World. In settled areas, the prodigality of the zigzag fence gave way to the more economical post-and-rail *(page 42)*, set directly on the property line. Still, the amount of lumber used in farm fences was staggering. By the end of the 19th Century, wooden fences were often worth more than the land they enclosed. An 1883 Iowa state agricultural report estimated that the United States' six million miles of wooden fences were worth two billion dollars—more than the national debt at the time.

Small wonder that when a cheap, convenient, durable substitute—barbed wire—became available, it began immediately to replace wood in farm fences. By the mid-1880s, a quarter of a million miles of barbed wire were being strung each year around American fields. Today, few farmers can afford to fence their acres with wood, and in most areas the last reminders of what was once characteristic of America's frontier agriculture are the post-and-rail fences decorating suburban lawns.

Building and Repairing Gates

A wooden fence gate is often an ornery object—indeed, the faulty ones sometimes seem to outnumber the good ones. They sag, they bind, they refuse to latch. But by following three simple precepts, you can have a gate as trouble-free as anyone can reasonably expect.

The first requirement is a pair of strong, plumb gateposts, set in concrete *(page 37)* to a depth equal to one half the height of the part aboveground. Space the posts to accommodate the gate width plus a ½-inch clearance for the latch as well as enough clearance for the kind of hinge you plan to install.

The second critical element is a frame that is braced by a diagonal board between the top rail at the latch side and the bottom rail at the hinge side. But no brace can sufficiently stiffen a gate wider than 5 feet; for a larger opening, install two gates. One gate is held closed with a cane bolt, a ½-inch sliding rod that drops through brackets on the edge of the gate into a hole in the pavement or in a block of concrete; the second gate latches to the first. To provide bottom clearance, hang all gates at least 1 inch above the highest point of ground within the arc of the opening gate.

The third crucial requirement is strong hardware, particularly the hinges *(below)*; weak hinges are the most frequent cause of gate problems. To prevent rusting, use cadmium-coated or galvanized hardware. Among latches, the simplest and most trouble-free are the thumb-and-string types; sliding bolts are not recommended because even a slight sag in the gate throws them out of alignment.

Even a carefully built gate may eventually sag and bind as its weight pulls hinge screws loose or causes the supporting post to lean. Problems of this nature are relatively easy to correct—leaning posts can be pulled upright with turnbuckles *(page 53, bottom)*; loose hinge screws can be either tightened or replaced.

To tighten screws, first take the gate off the post and, using a twist drill, enlarge the width of the old screw holes to ½ inch and drill the holes to a depth that is three fourths of the thickness of the post. Cut ½-inch dowels to the depth of the holes, coat them with waterproof glue and tap them into the holes with a mallet. Then drill holes in the dowels, ¹⁄₁₆ inch smaller than the screws, and rehang the gate. For an inexpensive improvement on this method, replace loose screws with bolts that go completely through the post and are secured by nuts on the other side. But it is best not to attempt repairs of basic damage, such as rot that severely weakens the wooden parts. It is easier to build a new gate instead.

How the hinges go on. These three common styles of hinge have one element in common: all attach to the gate with a strap, which should be at least 7 inches long. But the method of attachment to the post varies. The strap hinge has a post strap—preferably one that runs the full width of the post. The T hinge has a roughly rectangular pad, resembling the crossbar on a T; for a 3½-by-3½-foot gate the pad should be at least 7 inches high and 2 inches wide. The screw-hook hinge has an L-shaped screw hook driven into the post; the hook should be at least ½ inch thick and the screw 4 inches long. The screw-hook hinge *(page 53, Step 3)* has special advantages. It permits easy removal of the gate for minor repairs, and it is the simplest to attach to a masonry wall—either insert a flat-shank hook into a mortar joint while the wall is being built or drive a screw hook into a lead anchor.

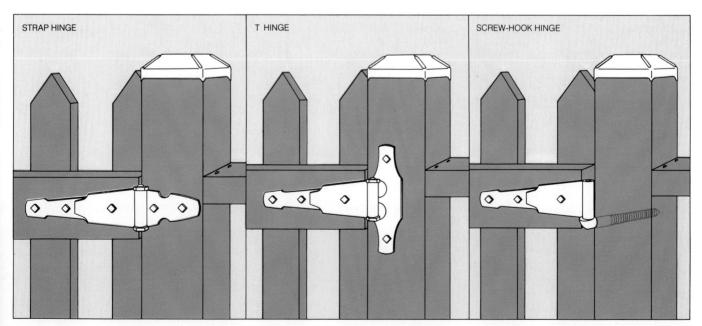

STRAP HINGE   T HINGE   SCREW-HOOK HINGE

Making and Hanging a Gate

1 **Assembling the frame.** Cut 2-by-4s the width of the gate for stringers and, using a steel square to guarantee right angles, nail pickets or 2-by-4s to the stringer ends. Position the pickets or rails so the stringers of the gate will align with those of the main fence. For a fence 6 feet tall or more, add a third rail or stringer at the middle of the frame. Before you proceed to the next step, nail both of the end pickets to the stringers, then turn the frame over.

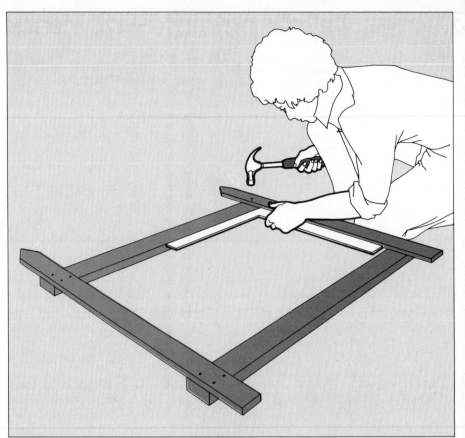

2 **Bracing the frame.** Mark and cut a 2-by-4 brace with angled ends to fit diagonally between the gate's top corner at the latch side and the bottom corner at the hinge side. Secure it with 4-inch wood screws started about 2 inches in from each end and angled into the stringers.

Nail the remaining pickets to the stringers and the brace. Fasten the hinge straps to the ends of the stringers with lag screws.

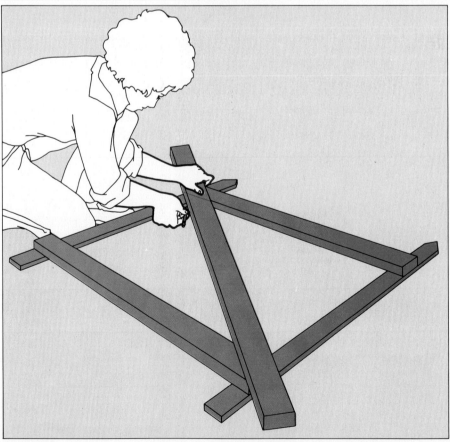

3 Hanging the gate. Set the gate on wood scraps to align it with the fence and, holding the back of the frame flush with the back of the post, mark the post at the bottom of the top hinge. Drive a screw hook diagonally into the post at the mark *(right inset)* and slip the hinge strap over the hook. Install the bottom screw hook in the same way and hang the gate.

To make a gatestop, nail a strip of 1-by-1½ flush with the front of the latch post. Install a latch bar on the gate and a latch on the post *(left inset)*. A string latch is shown here; most gate latches are installed in the same way.

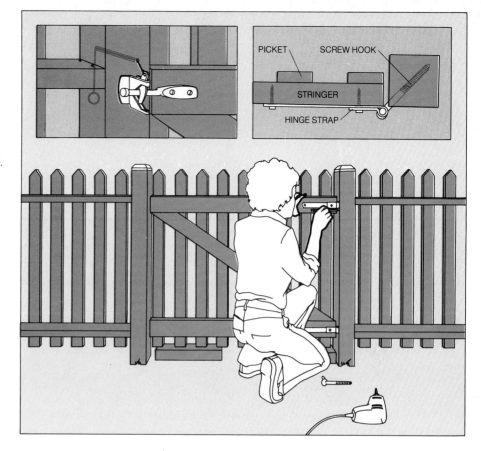

Remedies for Sags

Plumbing a leaning post. Pull the post to vertical with two ⅛-inch stainless-steel cables and a 7¾-inch turnbuckle fitted with ⅜-inch eyes. With cable clamps, secure one end of each cable to a ⅜-inch eyebolt, one at the top of the gatepost and the other at the bottom of the nearest fence post. Similarly secure the other ends of the cables to the turnbuckle *(inset)*, then tighten the turnbuckle by turning it with a screwdriver.

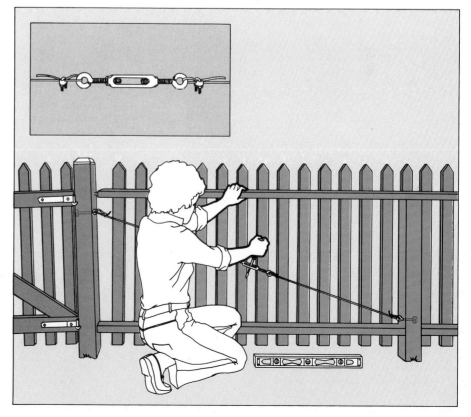

Blocks and Bricks for a Strong High Wall

Masonry walls make the most permanent of all fences, capable of taking nature's punishment for generations. Yet for all their sturdiness, they need not be forbidding ramparts. Softened by greenery or enlivened by patterns *(pages 61-63)*, even a massive 6-foot wall of brick or blocks can be a graceful garden ornament as well as a property boundary, a windbreak or a guardian of privacy.

Because of its solidity and weight, a masonry wall calls for more careful planning than other fences. It must sit on soil firm enough to support it, and not block natural drainage. If you have any doubts about the site of your wall, consult your local building authority. Check with utility companies about pipe and wire locations before digging the wall's foundation, and take special care not to violate property lines or local codes governing setback distances.

In addition to careful initial planning, a high masonry wall requires care and some skill in its construction if it is to be safely sturdy; an amateur attempting one should first gain experience with the basic masonry techniques. In many areas, codes prescribe strict standards for masonry structures more than a few feet high, specifying materials, dimensions, and depths of footings—the underground masses of solid concrete that support the structures.

Footings must be at least 18 inches below grade and must rest on earth not affected by frost. In much of North America, digging beyond the frost line to the level specified by the codes requires moving large amounts of soil. If you live in an area with severe winters and plan to build a high wall more than a dozen feet long, have the digging for the footing done by a professional with a backhoe. If a backhoe cannot be maneuvered into position, or if the amount of earth to be moved is comparatively small, consider renting a gasoline-powered trencher, which you can operate yourself.

Before you begin digging, mark the borders of the footing trench and the center line of the fence on the ground with a trickle of sand; drive stakes clear of the digging area to fix the marks. Allow space for dumping the moved earth—next to the trench and on your own property. Remember that in loose soil, you may have to bank the walls of the trench back from the bed by as much as 45° to keep them from caving in. Keep the bed as level and flat as you can, but do not smooth it off by filling loose earth back in: the footing must rest on undisturbed earth. If the virgin soil at the proper depth is loose, tamp it.

A footing's width and height depend on the thickness of the structure it supports. For a building foundation, normally 8 inches thick, the footing should be at least 16 inches wide and 8 inches high. For the brick wall on pages 57-60, which requires sections 16 inches thick, the footing should be heavier: about 24 inches wide and 10 inches deep.

In any but the loosest soil, you will not need wooden forms to pour concrete for a footing. In most soils, you should widen the trench on one side for room to smooth the concrete and lay blocks and mortar from the footing up to the surface. But if the soil is firm enough to keep the trench walls vertical for their full height, you have a convenient but expensive alternative: you can dig the whole trench no wider than the footing and fill it with concrete to a level just below the ground *(below, right)*.

Either kind of footing requires horizontal reinforcement—two lines of No. 4 steel bars laid along the trench—and either will probably need enough concrete for an order from a ready-mix firm. Explain what you need the concrete for and ask for an appropriate mix.

When the truck arrives, have plenty of helpers on hand. Pouring and leveling concrete is heavy work that must be done quickly. A fully loaded cement mixer weighs as much as 30 tons and may crack a driveway or rut a lawn. If you cannot bring the truck close enough to the trench to pour the concrete directly into it, use wheelbarrows equipped with pneumatic tires to ferry the concrete from the truck. When the concrete is poured and leveled, cover it with plastic sheeting and let it cure for 24 hours before starting to build on it.

Readying a Solid Footing

Two types of deep footing. The trenches at right contain two types of poured-concrete footing. The trench at near right, suitable for average soils, has one wall as nearly vertical as the firmness of the soil allows; the bottom is squared off to the width and height of the footing, and above that the trench gets a foot or two wider to create a shelf for working space. Reinforcing bars are laid, concrete is poured and leveled, then a block foundation is built up to within a few inches of ground level. The trench at far right, dug in very firm soil, has vertical walls separated by the width of the footing. Reinforcement is laid and the trench is filled with concrete almost to the surface; it needs no block foundation.

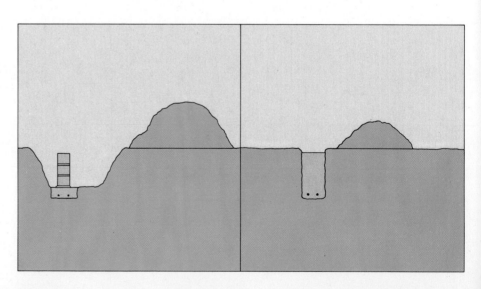

Placing the Concrete

1 **Leveling the bed.** At 3- to 4-foot intervals, drive parallel rows of 12-inch stakes a few inches into the ground along each side of the bed of the footing trench. Choose one stake at a high spot in the bed, mark it at a point 8 to 10 inches above the bed; then, using clear plastic tubing by the method shown on page 10, mark all the stakes at the same level.

2 **Driving the grade pegs.** Next to each stake, drive a grade peg—an 18-inch length of reinforcing bar—so that its top is exactly level with the mark on the stake. Be careful not to drive the pegs too deep. Remove the stakes and tamp the earth around each peg. Check the levels of the pegs with a 4-foot mason's level or a carpenter's level taped to a straight length of 2-by-4. If a peg is high, tap it lightly to drive it deeper.

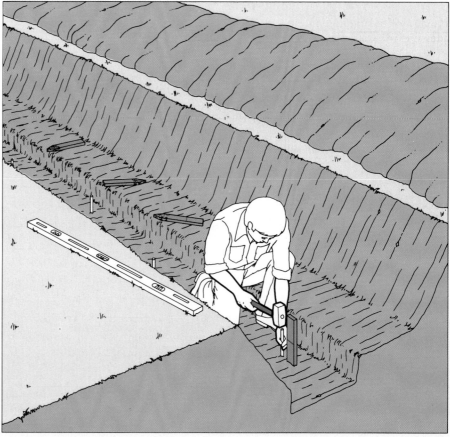

3 **Laying reinforcing bars.** Set lengths of No. 4 reinforcing bar alongside each row of grade pegs, supporting the bars 2 to 3 inches above the trench bed on bricks or stones. Where two bars meet, overlap them 12 to 15 inches, and use tie wire to lash the overlapping bars to each other and to the grade pegs.

4 **Completing the footing.** Working with helpers, pour concrete into the trench and spread it with square-tipped shovels, digging into it to break up air pockets. When the grade pegs are covered by at least ½ inch of concrete, level the footing with floats made from 2-by-4s nailed together to form a handle and a working surface. Covering a small area at a time, use a patting motion to compact the concrete until the tops of the grade pegs appear. Next, zigzag the floats horizontally until the surface of the concrete is fairly smooth, and finally sweep the surface with the trailing edge of the float, pulling it toward you in wide arcs. When you finish, the tops of the grade pegs should be barely visible at the surface of the concrete.

Extra-deep Footings: The Professional Approach

If you must provide a footing deeper than 3 feet, it is best to have a professional do the job. Just moving the earth for such a deep trench is a formidable project, and once it is dug, its sides must be shored up for the safety of the people who will work in it. For a wall 8 inches thick, a footing 8 inches high and 16 inches wide is poured in the bottom of a trench with a notch or key running its length—to stabilize the foundation on top of it—and vertical reinforcing bars projecting up from it, to strengthen the aboveground part of the wall. Then a wooden form *(below)* is generally built above the footing in order to cast a foundation 8 inches thick up to ground level. Once both sections of concrete have been poured and cured, forms are removed and the construction of the wall can begin.

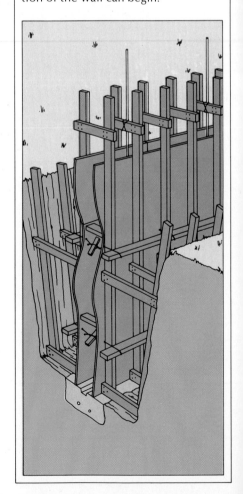

56

Laying Blocks and Bricks

In addition to deep footings, high masonry walls need lateral support. A freestanding garden wall 8 inches thick and more than 4 feet high should be braced against winds and climbing children. It can be supported with pilasters—thick columns built into the wall—to give it a broader base, or with vertical steel bars embedded in the footing. The 8-inch walls shown on these pages are reinforced with square pilasters that are 16 inches on a side. Their footings are 24 inches wide and 10 inches deep.

Regardless of the type of wall you are planning aboveground, it is most economical to build from the top of the footing up to ground level with inexpensive masonry block. You will need standard "stretcher" blocks measuring 8 by 8 by 16 inches, together with a few half blocks measuring 8 by 8 by 8 inches, to avoid having to cut the large stretchers; flat-ended "double-corner" blocks, and "partition" blocks measuring 4 by 8 by 16 inches for the pilasters. Have all the blocks delivered on pallets if possible, and keep them covered with plastic sheeting—blocks must be laid dry.

A few inches below ground level, begin laying the masonry units for the wall itself. For a brick wall like the one on the following pages, the number of standard-sized bricks you will need equals 14 times the area of one face of the wall in square feet, with an extra 90 for each 6-foot pilaster. You will also need enough half blocks to fill the cores of the pilasters (9 or 10 for each in a 6-foot wall), and four solid bricks for each pilaster cap.

Pilasters should be spaced 8 to 12 feet apart; try to make the total length of the wall and the distance between pilasters divisible by 8 inches to facilitate brick-and-block construction. The cores of the blocks in the pilasters should be grouted with concrete—not mortar—from the footing up. For added strength, run two 6-foot lengths of No. 4 reinforcing bar down to the footing through the cores of the foundation blocks in each pilaster before grouting them full. Keep in mind that a pilaster is useful as a wall support only if it is perfectly plumb, which requires scrupulous checking with a level.

1 Aligning the blocks. Snap two chalk lines along the footing, one 4 inches from its center to mark the edge of the bottom course of blocks for the wall, and another 4 inches outside the first to mark the edge of the pilasters. Lay a dry run of the first course to the chalk lines, with a pair of blocks at each pilaster. Leave a ⅜-inch space between the ends of the blocks to allow for the mortar joints. Adjust the thickness of the joints to bring the course to the correct length. Mark the location of each pilaster with chalk on the footing.

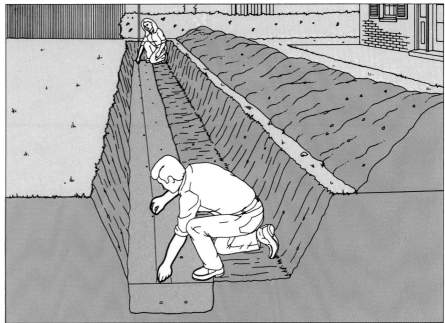

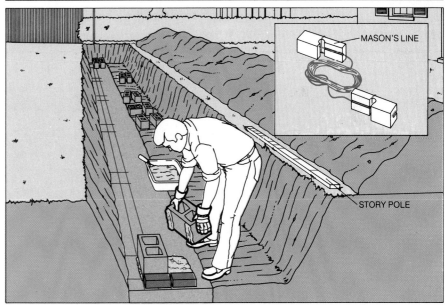

MASON'S LINE

STORY POLE

2 First course. At the marks for one of the end pilasters, lay two double-corner blocks side by side in a full mortar bed. Gauge how much space to leave between the blocks by placing two bricks end to end across the footing, with the end of one brick at the outside chalk line, and ⅜ inch between the bricks. Lay the blocks so that their outside edges are even with the ends of the bricks. This will leave about an inch between the blocks; the space should be empty. Check both blocks for plumb and level with a mason's level; check the height of their mortar bed with a story pole—a homemade measuring stick marked where the top of each course should be when its mortar joint is the right thickness.

Lay two more double-corner blocks for the other end pilaster, run a mason's line (inset) between the two ends and lay pairs of similar blocks for the other pilasters to the line. Fill their cores with concrete.

3 Completing the first course. Lay a stretcher block in mortar inside each end pilaster and on both sides of the other pilasters, centering the stretcher blocks on the joint between the two pilaster blocks—use the inside chalk line as a guide. After the mortar has begun to set, use two line pins stuck in the vertical joints between the pilasters and the stretcher blocks to run a mason's line to establish a guideline for the rest of the stretchers to be laid between each pair of pilasters. Fill in the blocks for each section and point up the holes in the mortar left by the line pins.

4 Completing the foundation. Begin the second course of blocks with a half block at each end, centered over the joint between the pilaster blocks. Lay a corner block inside each half block, run a mason's line from one end to the other and fill in between them with ordinary stretcher blocks. Next, lay partition blocks at the end pilasters, sandwiching the newly laid second-course blocks as shown below. Three sides of the stretcher blocks must be plumb with the paired double-corner blocks beneath them. Make similar sandwiches at the other pilasters with the aid of a mason's line run from the ends. For the third course, repeat the first, but at each pilaster set a 15-inch length of truss-type joint reinforcement across the wall embedded in the mortar before laying the blocks.

When the mortar has set, fill the openings in the blocks at each pilaster with concrete so that there is a continuous column of concrete from the footing up to a few inches from the top of the third course. If you plan to use vertical reinforcing bars, thread them down through the blocks to the footing before grouting and tie them in place until the concrete sets.

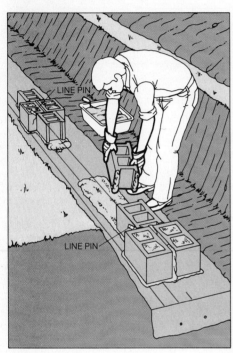

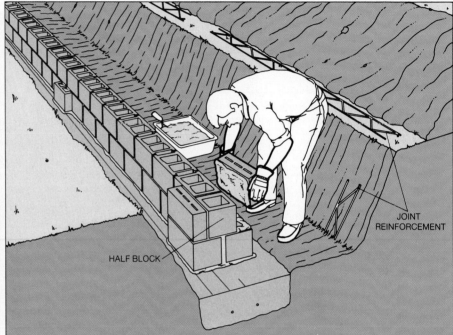

5 A dry run. With the foundation built up almost to ground level, lay a dry run of the first course of bricks to adjust their fit from pilaster to pilaster. Lay the bricks in the pattern shown at right and set a half block at the core of each pilaster. The bricks in the pilasters should be plumb with the blocks beneath them on three sides; keep any overlap on one side as shown. Between pilasters, separate two rows of bricks so that a brick laid across them fits plumb. Separated in this way, the two rows of bricks should overlap the single row of blocks they rest on. Keep all the overlap on one side of the wall so that the other side can be plumbed up from the foundation.

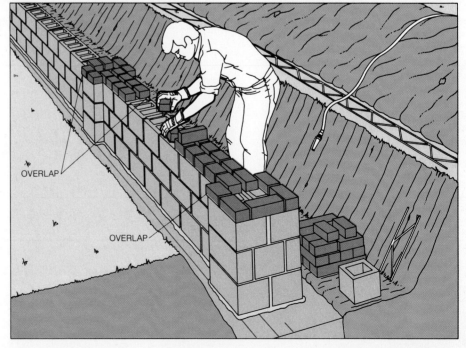

6 **Laying the first bricks.** Start by building a lead—the end structure—six courses high at one end of the wall. Spread mortar on the tops of the blocks of the end pilaster and on 2½ feet of the adjoining wall. Set a 10-foot length of joint reinforcement in the mortar, starting an inch from the wall's end. Using the dry-run pattern, lay well-moistened bricks around the pilaster rim and three and a half brick lengths out onto the wall. Set a half block in the middle of the pilaster; double-check each brick for level and plumb.

Mortar the tops of the first-course bricks and lay the second course one half brick shorter than the first, varying the pattern as shown to avoid lining up vertical joints. The third course repeats the pattern of the first, stepped back one half brick from the second. The top of the third course should be level with the top of the block in the center of the pilaster; set a 15-inch length of joint reinforcement across the pilaster in the mortar on top of the third course and proceed with the next three courses, checking repeatedly for level and plumb. Alternate the pattern and shorten the lead one half brick in each course. Build a similar lead at the other end pilaster.

7 **Building up the pilasters.** At the pilasters between ends, build six-course double leads—ones that step up from the wall on both sides. Start with 10-foot lengths of joint reinforcement in the mortar on top of the block foundation; overlap their ends 12 to 15 inches. Lay bricks in a pattern similar to that used for the end pilasters, but with leads extending out onto the wall from both sides. Use a mason's line strung from the end pilasters to maintain alignment. Fill the cores of the blocks in the centers of the pilasters with concrete as in Step 4. Complete the courses between the pilasters, running a mason's line from line pins stuck in the vertical mortar joints next to the pilasters as in Step 3.

You should now have a solid wall six courses high; on both sides of the foundation, fill in the dirt dug out for the footing trench and tamp it well.

8 **Extending the wall upward.** Lay joint reinforcement along the wall on top of the sixth course and build new six-course leads at each pilaster as before. Grout the cores, fill in between the pilasters and repeat. If you lay one or two courses of brick below grade, four six-course leads will take the wall to 5 feet; three more courses plus a cap will take it to 6 feet.

9 **Capping the wall.** When the wall is 4 inches short of the height you want, lay joint reinforcement along the top, build the pilasters up three more courses and fill their cores. Lay a cap of rowlocks (bricks laid on edge) along the wall between the pilasters. Start with a dry run to see whether you will have to adjust the thicknesses of the joints for a proper fit.

10 **Capping the pilasters.** For each pilaster, cut eight 1-inch-thick pieces of brick (that is, pieces measuring 1 by 2¼ by 4 inches), called closers, to use in widening the cap courses. Following the basic pilaster pattern, lay the first course of the cap with full-sized bricks around the rim of the pilaster so that they project an inch over the edge on all sides. Fit four of the closer pieces between the whole bricks, one on each side, to fill out the course. Set two bricks in the middle of the pilaster and fill all the space around them with mortar.

Alternating the pattern, lay the second cap course plumb with the first. Put two more bricks in the center and grout solid with mortar. For the final course, lay a double rowlock cap across the pilaster, set in from the course beneath in the original dimensions, 16 by 16 inches.

Decorative Masonry Patterns

Masonry walls need not always present a solid, unvarying face. Brick and block can be laid in patterns to enliven a wall's appearance and in open designs to admit light and air while screening a view.

Decorative patterns for walls made of blocks, particularly those with openings, most often use a form of stacked bond: the units do not overlap but have their vertical joints lined up. The lack of overlapping joints weakens the wall, which therefore requires strengthening with joint reinforcement and steel bars *(top right)*. Horizontal joint reinforcement should be embedded in the mortar along the full length of the wall after every second or third course of blocks—after each course with 12-inch screen blocks. Where hollow cores of blocks align vertically, reinforcing bars at 4-foot intervals can be run from the footing up through the blocks halfway up the wall.

The block patterns shown on page 62 use stacked bond and blocks of widely available, standard sizes. Odd sizes give you more complex patterns, but whatever the pattern, arrange blocks so that continuous reinforcement can be laid between courses and so that very few blocks stand on end, the position in which they weaken the wall most.

Bricks can also be used to make openwork, but such walls require a skilled mason to make them structurally sound. An amateur bricklayer, however, can build a solid brick wall with a decorative pattern based on the interplay of headers (bricks laid crosswise on the wall) and stretchers (bricks laid along the length of the wall). Such designs strengthen an ordinary two-course-thick garden wall, since the headers tie the front and back courses of brick together, performing part of the function of joint reinforcement.

Most traditional brick patterns are developed either from English bond, in which courses of headers and stretchers alternate *(center right)*, or from Flemish bond, which has alternating headers and stretchers in each course *(bottom right)*. Variations of these two bonds will produce an enormous range of ornamental patterns, which can be heightened by using bricks of contrasting colors.

A large brickyard will stock from 20 to 30 different colors of brick, but for a simple design like those shown, you need only two colors of standard-faced building bricks, one for a background and the other for the pattern. Buy all the bricks at once: colors vary from lot to lot, and you may not be able to match bricks later.

To determine how many bricks you need in each color, diagram the pattern on graph paper. Make each course one square high; let two horizontal squares represent a header and four squares a stretcher. Diagram enough complete courses (usually two or three) to show the bond pattern, count the number of odd-colored bricks in these courses and multiply the figure by the number of pattern repeats you will need for the entire wall. Double the number of odd-colored stretchers if you want the pattern to show on both sides of a wall two courses thick; add the odd-colored headers and subtract the total from the number of bricks needed for the whole wall *(page 57)*. Buy 5 per cent extra bricks in both colors to allow for breakage.

When you design a wall with one of the pattern units shown in the center and right rows on page 63, you must design it from the center to make the pattern symmetrical, though you will actually build the wall from its ends. On graph paper, draw an outline of a full section of the wall. Make the wall an odd number of courses high—the course that serves as a horizontal axis for the design must have an even number of courses above and below it. Find the squares that represent the center brick of the section. Fill in the pattern unit over this center brick, then fill in the rest of the section. You can now tell how many pattern units or parts of units will fit into the section and the wall, and how to begin laying the bricks.

The diagram will also show that to make a design with Flemish bond or English bond, alternate courses must begin and end with either a quarter brick, called a queen closer *(bottom right)*, or a three-quarter brick, called a king closer *(center right)*. The odd sizes can be made by setting bricks more or less than halfway into a pilaster or by cutting bricks. If you cut queen closers, locate them near—but not at—the end of a course. To save time, cut all the closers before you start laying bricks.

Reinforcing stacked blocks. Walls of stacked bond need both horizontal and vertical reinforcement. The pilasters bracing the wall below are cross pairs of double-corner blocks knitted to the rest of the wall with continuous stretches of joint reinforcement laid after every second course. No. 4 steel rods run up through the cores of the blocks of each pilaster and at 4-foot intervals between pilasters. The cores with the rods are filled with concrete.

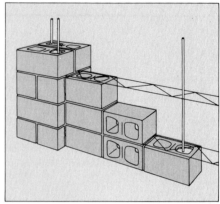

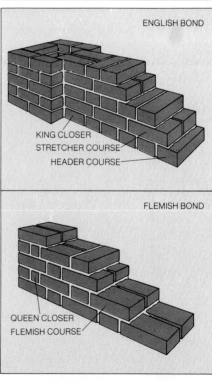

ENGLISH BOND

KING CLOSER
STRETCHER COURSE
HEADER COURSE

FLEMISH BOND

QUEEN CLOSER
FLEMISH COURSE

Basic ornamental bonds. In English bond *(top)*, header and stretcher courses alternate; in Flemish bond *(above)*, each course consists of alternating header and stretcher bricks. Quarter or three-quarter bricks (closers) are used at or near the ends of courses to align the headers and stretchers in every other course.

Open and Shut Designs with Blocks

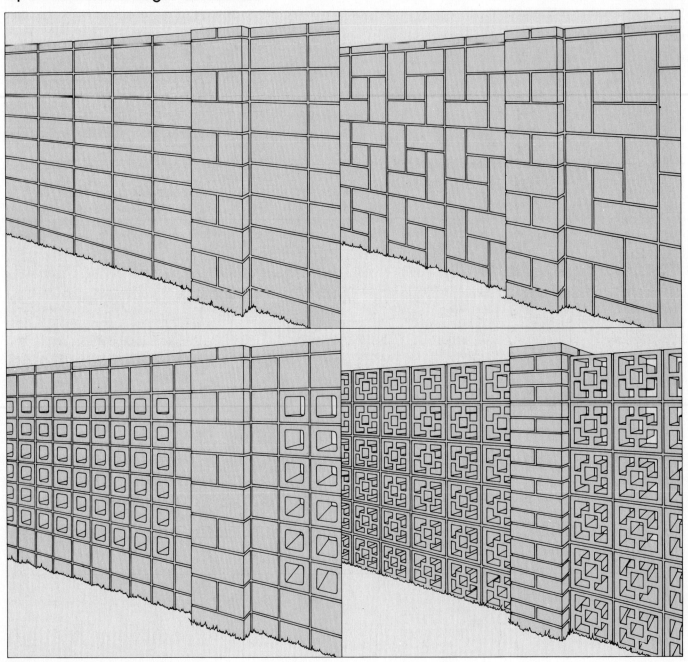

Decorative walls from blocks. Ordinary stretcher blocks in stacked bond *(top, left)* make a surprisingly good-looking wall; the cap course is of flat, coreless block. A basket-weave pattern *(top, right)* is made from units of four stretchers and a half block. More half blocks laid on their sides *(above, left)* can be arranged in a wide variety of patterns to form openings for light and air. Ornamental 12-inch screen blocks *(above, right)* require half-high blocks (4 by 8 by 16 inches) for pilasters so that horizontal reinforcement can be laid atop each course. The pilasters are capped and the mortar is packed in the vertical joints of the top course.

Fancy Tricks with Colored Bricks

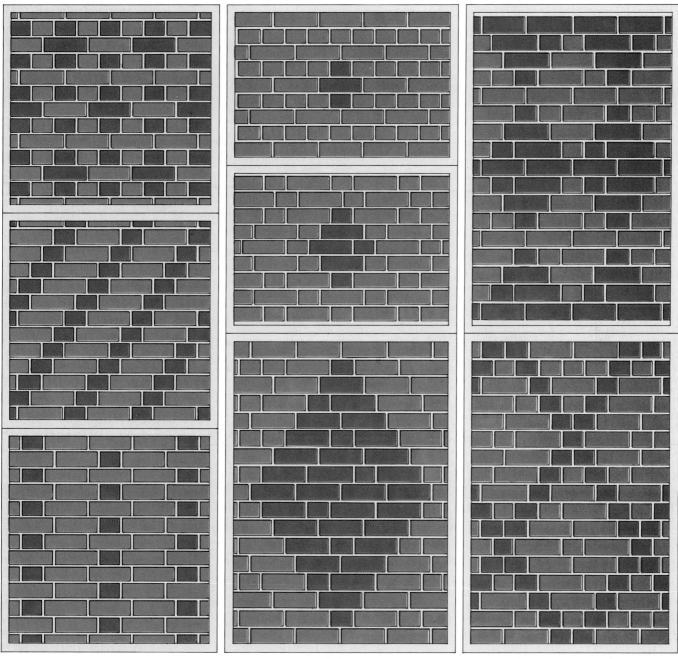

English and Flemish variations. Bricks in contrasting colors, and courses in which brick overlaps are offset, give the two ornamental bonds a different look. In English cross bond *(top)*, a variation of English bond, the stretcher bricks "cross," or "break joint"—that is, they overlap one another by a half brick in succeeding courses. Color emphasizes the pattern: stretcher courses are alternately of a single color and two contrasting colors. In Flemish spiral bond *(center)*, a pattern of diagonal bands is created by the placement of dark crossed headers. Garden-wall bond *(above)* consists of Flemish courses in which every fourth brick is a header.

Making a pattern unit. More complex designs are based on pattern units called eyes. The fundamental eye *(top)* consists of a single stretcher with headers centered above and below it. Larger eyes are formed by extending the unit by the width of one header in each course, adding headers at the top and bottom and centering the whole on the middle, or axis, course *(center)*. You can expand the primary unit in this way until it assumes a clear diamond shape *(above)*.

Combining pattern units. Large wall designs consist of a number of pattern units defined by colored bricks and arranged to cover the wall symmetrically. In one widely used design *(top)*, the eyes butt one another, forming horizontal bands, and the bands are emphasized by a course of solid-color stretchers between the rows of eyes. Colored borders can make a simple pattern unit into a more complex design: in the example above, each unit is bordered by dark headers.

A Thin, Yet Sinuously Solid Wall

Grace in masonry. An 1887 drawing depicts an alley on the University of Virginia campus leading to a colonnade and bordered by two of Jefferson's winding walls. An inset shows Jefferson's plan for a series of gardens surrounded by serpentine walls.

To the sharp, inquiring eye of Thomas Jefferson, the graceful serpentine walls he viewed on a tour of famous English gardens in the late 1780s were both alluring and ingenious. Jefferson was attracted to the obvious beauty of the walls—called "crinkle-crankle" in England—but also to their subtle economy. Unlike traditional masonry walls, the serpentine design needed no buttressing pilasters and no double layer of bricks, deriving its strength from its built-in curves.

Jefferson saw the serpentine wall as a delightful addition to his plan to blend Old World forms into the grounds of the University of Virginia, and to create a neoclassical "Academical Village" embowered by gardens. In England, he wrote, plants thrived at the bases of serpentine walls, because the walls' curves focused the sun's warmth. Their rippling shadows pleased the eye of the late-afternoon stroller.

To Jefferson's pragmatic mind—he kept track of the budget for the construction of the university, and paid special attention to the price of brick, which he found to be "exorbitant"—the economy of serpentine walls was as important as their aesthetic value. He calculated that although a serpentine wall was longer than a straight one spanning the same distance, it required only about two thirds the number of bricks.

The serpentine design is as useful and economical now as it was in the 18th Century. It consists of a series of identical curves in a wavelike pattern. The trick now as then is to make the height of the wall consistent with the degree of curvature. As the British masons whose work Jefferson admired had discovered, the higher the wall, the more it had to undulate to maintain itself. A low wall could be built in a series of shallow curves; for a higher wall, the curves had to be tighter and to extend farther out from the wall's center line.

Modern masons have reduced these considerations to two handy rules of thumb: the radius of the curves should be less than twice the proposed height of the wall, and the total width of the wall should be more than half the wall's proposed height.

Thus, a serpentine wall with a height of 4 feet above ground level would have to be built in curves that had a radius of 8 feet or less and a total width of at least 2 feet. In some parts of the country where high winds prevail, local building codes might require that the wall be built with even tighter curves.

Turning a corner is a fairly simple matter; as the bricklayer arrives at the corner, he merely continues the curve on which he is working until the corner is turned, then continues his pattern in the new direction.

Ironically, Jefferson's own serpentine walls did not stand. In the 1800s, university administrators complained that the walls were in constant need of repair, and by the turn of the century hardly any were still standing. In 1949 the Garden Club of Virginia undertook the reconstruction of the walls. Following the old ground plans, landscape architects working on the project located some of the original foundations, and were able to rebuild all the serpentine walls exactly where Jefferson had planned them.

Try as they might, though, the architects were unable to explain why the original walls had fallen down. They conjectured that the bricklayers had not mixed enough crushed oyster shells—a source of lime—into the mortar.

Putting In Metal Fences

Ornamental "iron" fences—which today are steel or aluminum—are among the strongest and most durable of open fences. They also tend to be among the most costly. New ones are generally custom-made at small ironworks, though less expensive prefabricated panels of aluminum or steel bars are available from some retail fence dealers in a limited range of sizes and styles. It is also possible to construct a low metal fence from prefabricated railing panels widely available at building-supply stores, but such a fence may not be much cheaper than one designed for the purpose.

Old metal fences may be the most desirable. They are made of virtually indestructible wrought iron in elaborate Victorian designs hard to duplicate today, but they are generally very expensive, and it may be hard to find one in decent condition that suits your property.

Installing a new metal fence yourself will save 20 to 30 per cent of the cost of one professionally installed—and if you order in winter, the slow season for ironworks, you may get a lower price. To order a custom-built fence, first consult with the ironworks and draw up a detailed profile of the fence and the terrain it is to cover. Precise measurements are essential: once the panels are assembled and welded, there is little room for adjustment. The profile (top right) should show the exact contour of the land and the key dimensions of the fence. If the ground is uneven, decide at this stage whether to level it or to have the fence follow the contours, either in steps (page 50) or by sloping the stringers.

Have the ironworks coat the fence with red oxide or zinc-chromate primer before delivery. Before you put it up, give it two coats of oil-based exterior paint.

Making the profile. Run a level string along the line of the fence. Measure the height of the string at the locations of the posts and of significant dips and rises in the ground. Record the profile of the terrain on graph paper and draw in the posts and panels to scale.

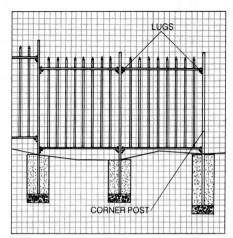

Note on the profile the height and length of panels and gates, the spacing and dimensions of the pickets and stringers, the thickness and total height of the posts (as much as one third must go belowground in concrete—page 34), the location of the lugs for bolting the panels to the posts, the locations of hinges and latches, and any additional ornamentation. For a stepped or sloped fence, note the size of the stringer drop (page 50) or the angle of the stringer slope.

Setting the posts and panels. Because of the precise tolerances of metal fences, posts are put up together with panels and the assembled units are plumbed and braced in position in the postholes. When the fence is delivered, dig postholes and put several inches of coarse gravel in each hole. Run a low string precisely along the line of the fence. Starting at an end, corner or gate, bolt posts to both sides of a panel and mark the posts with chalk to show how much should be set above grade.

Place both posts, with the panel in place between them, in their holes just inside the string, supporting the panel with blocks under the bottom stringer. Adjust the gravel in the holes until it supports the posts at the correct height and the panel is level or properly sloped. Plumb each post and brace the panel from both sides with notched 2-by-4s nailed to stakes.

Bolt a third post to the next panel and attach the free end to the braced panel. Level, plumb and brace as before, repeating the procedure until all the fence is up and secure. At gates, set and brace a gatepost and panel on one side of a gate opening, then mount the gate to locate the other gatepost and panel. Before filling the holes with concrete (page 37), check once more to see that all posts are plumb and aligned.

3

Quick-and-Easy Backyard Building

Ready for installation. Coverings suitable for sheathing light outdoor structures range from rolls of woven reed and lengths of bamboo to conventional screening and a crisscrossing framework of wooden lattice. Designed for openness, these materials are so light in weight that in most cases all you need for fastening them to a structure is an ordinary staple gun.

Like Kubla Khan decreeing a stately pleasure dome, you can embellish your backyard Xanadu with a truly spectacular dome—or with a shed, an arbor, a tree house or a gazebo. But unlike the subject of Coleridge's famous poem, you can carry out the decree personally and build the structure yourself. Moreover, you can build it with a minimum of time, labor and expense, since unlike the great Khan, you have available an astonishing variety of techniques. They make possible structures that, while not built for the ages, are sturdy enough to last for as long as you will want to use them.

Of the many methods available for building the quick-and-easy structures shown on the following pages, some, like the post-and-beam, are older than the Pyramids; others, like the geodesic dome, are recent adaptations of ancient forms. But for all of them, you begin by erecting a skeleton. To build an A-frame, for example, you first erect inverted Vs of jointed timbers to serve as ribs of the combination roof-walls. Similarly, with post-and-beam buildings, you first raise the posts and then link them with horizontal beams. This technique—which man developed for his first wooden dwellings, refined for the Parthenon and still uses for skyscrapers—is strong, yet leaves large open spaces between the supports.

A structural skeleton alone may be enough for an arbor, but for a shade house you may want to add a partial covering and for a storage shed you need a weatherproof skin. Sheathing materials often do double duty: traditional wood and plywood combine sheathing with weatherproofing. Decorative lattice, bamboo, and woven-reed coverings also moderate the glare of sun and blast of wind. Easily installed screens keep out bugs but let in air and sunshine. Inexpensive plastic panels repel wind and water but admit light.

When you imaginatively combine decorative sheathings with fanciful frames, the whole structure becomes fun. The gazebo, a multisided post-and-beam structure, lends itself to the addition of lattices, curlicues and cupolas. As for tree houses, only the fertile imagination of youth is needed to convert an arboreal platform into a castle, a space ship or a frigate's quarter-deck.

One type of lightweight structure is not an offspring of traditional construction at all, but the brain child of a 20th Century genius who figured out how to weave a web of triangles into the shape of the age-old hemispherical dome. Buckminster Fuller's geodesic domes are based on the geometric shape called an icosahedron. Yet advanced mathematics plays no great role in dome-building—you can erect this lacing of struts as readily as a square shed, and people will admire your many-faceted pleasure dome even if they have never heard its technical name.

The A-Frame: Modern Tent Built with Plywood

One of the simplest of all buildings takes the form of a braced triangle—an A-frame—rising from the ground. Nailed together at the peak of an A-frame, the rafters that serve as both roof and walls enclose a structure that is practical for many types of small outdoor buildings. A low A-frame, with a peak 3 to 5 feet above the ground, might be used as a pet shelter or a storage shed; a higher one, with 6 or more feet of headroom, can serve as a garden house or a playroom.

In every A-frame, the walls that form the roof are equal, but the angle at the peak may vary considerably, and this angle affects both headroom and floor space. A typical A-frame, like the one on

these pages, is an equilateral triangle, with a base and sides of exactly the same length. A-frames with steeper sides have more headroom, but proportionately less floor space; flattening the triangle has the opposite effect.

Before you begin to build, decide upon the slope of the A-frame and, using a framing square *(page 70, Step 2),* mark angle cuts at the peak and bottom of each rafter. The slope is the ratio of the rise (the vertical distance from the base to the peak) to the run (the distance between the midpoint and the end of the base), expressed in inches of rise for every 12 inches of run. The roof of the A-frame on these pages has a slope of 21

in 12, but the framing square can mark rafter angles for any slope you choose.

The rafters of an A-frame, like those of any two-sided roof, must be reinforced to prevent spreading and sagging. In a small A-frame resting directly on the ground or on a bed of gravel, you can brace the rafters with crossties (called collar beams). In structures where headroom is valued, the horizontal reinforcements can be built into the floor. If you intend to use your A-frame for storage alone, simply bolt the rafters to a reinforced concrete slab *(below).* In garden shelters or playhouses, sandwich the rafters between wooden joists *(opposite, top),* and install flooring *(pages 100-101).*

A Compact, Triangular Structure

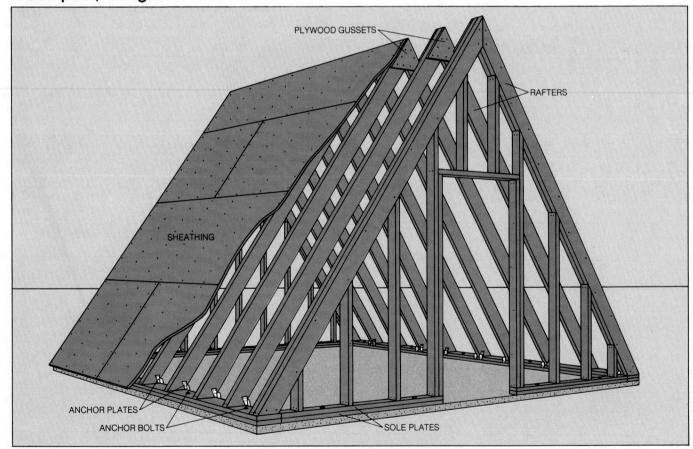

Anatomy of an A-frame. The rafters of this typical A-frame are 2-by-6s joined at their peaks with triangular plywood gussets (the gussets on the outermost rafters are omitted so that sheathing will lie flat against the vertical walls). The bases of the rafters are fastened by metal anchor plates, and the sole plates on all four sides are bolted to a concrete slab. At the ends of the A-frame the vertical sides are framed with conventional 2-by-4 sole plates and studding, and the entire structure is covered with plywood boards and weatherproof sheathing.

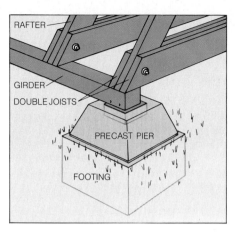

RAFTER

GIRDER

DOUBLE JOISTS

PRECAST PIER

FOOTING

Piers for a wooden floor. At the corners, concrete footings 12 inches thick, ⅜-inch mortar beds and precast concrete piers serve as a foundation for 4-by-4 girders and 2-by-6 joists in an A-frame with a wooden floor. The girders, which are adequate for spans of up to 4½ feet, are toenailed to wood nailing blocks that fit into precast cavities in the tops of the piers; the joists, in turn, are toenailed to the girders and fastened to the rafters with ⅝-inch machine bolts. The joists sandwiched around each rafter will brace the walls of the A-frame and provide a solid base for the flooring. For an A-frame with rafters that span more than 4½ feet, use doubled 2-by-6s, on edge, for girders.

Laying the Foundation

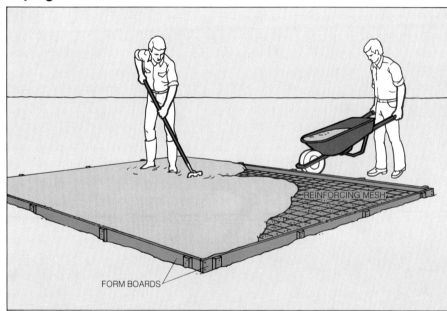

REINFORCING MESH

FORM BOARDS

1 Pouring the concrete. Empty the concrete for a small slab into a rectangular wooden form of 1-by-6 boards staked into the ground and enclosing a 6-inch-thick bed of gravel covered by 10-guage 6 × 6 wire reinforcing mesh (page 110). Use a mortar hoe to pack each load up against the preceding one, until the concrete comes just over the top edge of the form.

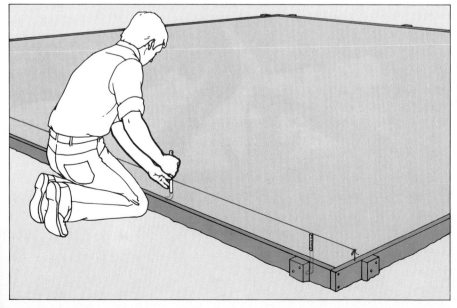

2 Placing anchor bolts. When the concrete begins to harden, embed 8-inch anchor bolts along the edges of the slab, leaving the top 4 inches of each bolt exposed above the concrete. Run a string along the sides of the slab 3¾ inches in from the edge and place the first bolt along the string, starting 8 inches from one end, and the remaining bolts at 32-inch intervals. On the front and back of the slab, place the first and last bolts 24 inches from the ends, the remaining ones at 32-inch intervals, 1¾ inches in from the edges, but leave a gap in the front row for a door.

When the concrete hardens, snap chalk lines 7½ inches from the sides of the slab and 3½ inches from the front and back to mark locations for the inner edges of the sole plates.

Building Roofs That Are Walls

1 Marking a sole plate. On each side of the slab, line up a 2-by-8 sole plate along the chalk line you snapped parallel to the anchor bolts and, using a framing square, transfer the positions of the bolts to the plate. To center the bolt-hole locations on the plate, measure the distance from the bolts to the edge of the plate and mark this distance off on the plate.

Mark the rafter locations on the plate between the bolt marks, setting the spacing for 16-inch centers and allowing for double rafters at both ends. Finally, set the plate on a second 2-by-8 cut to the same length, drill through both plates at the spots marked for anchor bolts and bolt the doubled plate in place on the slab.

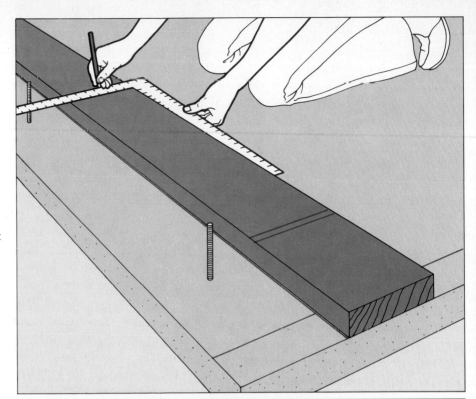

2 Marking angle cuts. Lay the framing square across a 2-by-6 rafter board so that the outside edges of the long and short arms—the body and the tongue—touch the edge of the board at the points that correspond to the slope of the A-frame; in this example, in which the slope is 21 in 12, the body of the square meets the edge of the board at the 21 mark, the tongue at the 12. Draw a line along the outer edge of the body to mark the cut for the rafter peak. To mark the cut for the rafter base, move the square down the board until the 12 mark on the tongue's outer edge meets the edge of the board at a point corresponding to the length of the A-frame side; realign the slope and draw a line along the outer edge of the tongue of the square (inset).

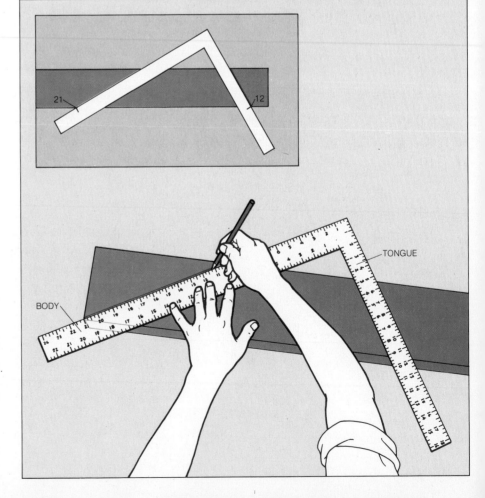

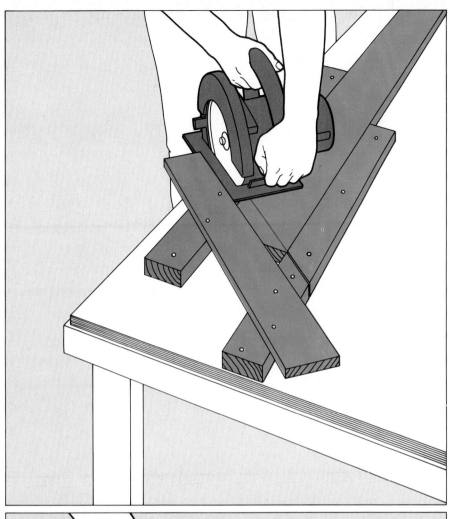

3 **Using a jig.** Saw the rafter-board ends with a circular saw in a homemade cutting jig consisting of two 2-by-4s nailed onto a plywood board. To make the jig, space the 2-by-4s 5½ inches apart (the width of a 2-by-6 rafter board). Slip the marked rafter board between the 2-by-4s and nail a 1-by-4 guide to them, at an angle that matches the angle cut you have marked for the top of the rafter. Check to be sure that the blade of the saw cuts along the rafter mark.

Use the jig to cut the bases of the rafter boards by realigning the 1-by-4 to match the angle you have cut for the rafter base.

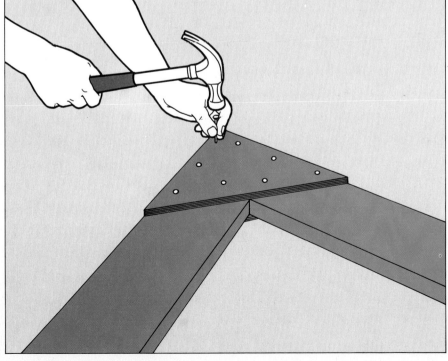

4 **A-joints.** Set pairs of rafters together on the ground to form roof peaks, and nail triangular plywood gussets on both sides of the peak joints, using exterior-grade ⅝-inch plywood cut to the same angle as the peak. Drive at least six four-penny nails in a triangular pattern to make the joint secure. Caution: do not nail gussets to the outsides of the front and back peaks.

5 **Setting the first A.** With a helper, raise a pair of double rafters into position over the marked locations at the end of the sole plate. Brace the rafters temporarily with a scrap 2-by-4 nailed to a stake about 5 feet from the slab. Use a carpenter's level to be sure the rafters are plumb.

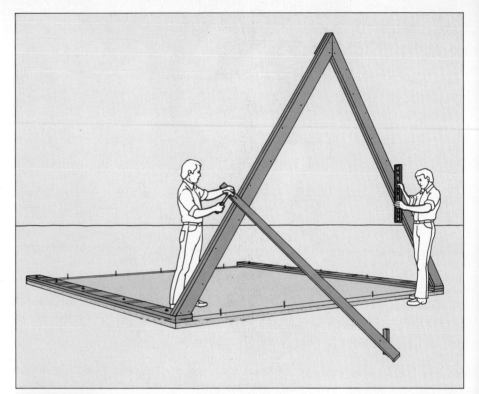

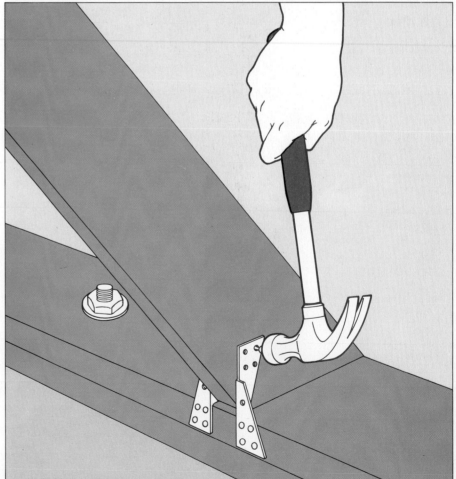

6 **Attaching the anchor plates.** Fasten rafters to the sole plates with metal anchor plates fastened to both sides of a rafter with fourpenny nails; for additional stability, toenail two eightpenny nails through the outside edge of the rafter into the sole plate. When you have anchored and plumbed three sets of rafters to the sole plate, install temporary stiffeners—horizontal 1-by-2s nailed into the rafter edges—to keep them steady.

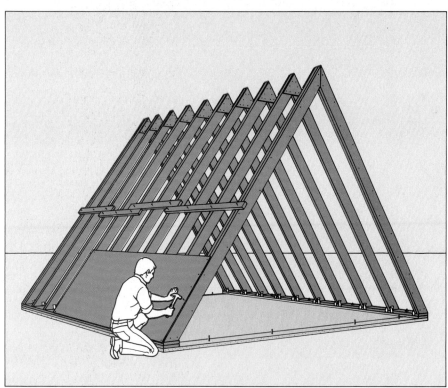

7 **Sheathing the rafters.** Nail 4-by-8 panels of ⅝-inch exterior plywood horizontally along the rafters. Begin at the outer edge and bottom of the first rafter. Nail the corners of a panel first, then nail through all the rafters beneath, spacing the nails 6 inches apart. After you have completed the bottom row of sheathing, remove the temporary stiffening and complete the rest of the side. Stagger the joints between plywood boards by cutting the first board of the second row to end at the midpoint of the board below.

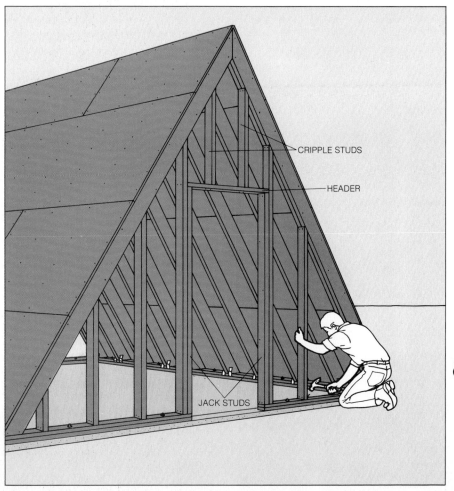

CRIPPLE STUDS

HEADER

JACK STUDS

8 **Studding the end walls.** Bolt doubled 2-by-4 sole plates to the anchor bolts at the front and back ends of the slab, then install studs for the front and back walls on 16-inch centers, toenailing each stud to the sole plate below and the rafter above. Leave a space for a door in the studding of the front wall; frame the space with jack studs, a header and cripple studs in the front wall. Saw off the sole plates in the door opening and sheathe the ends of the A-frame.

Post-and-Beam: An Old Method Resurrected

As homeowners spend more time in their backyards—and desire structures that make gardens more enjoyable—they are discovering the advantages of post-and-beam construction. For the supporting framework, it uses a few big pieces of lumber, widely spaced, instead of the many closely spaced 2-by-4 studs, stiffened with sheathing, normally employed today for homebuilding. The standard construction method until the early 19th Century, when machine-made nails and mill-sawed lumber made the stud wall more economical, post-and-beam is particularly adapted for outdoor uses.

To construct a post-and-beam framework, you anchor two parallel rows of wooden posts, connect the posts in each row with crossbeams to form a wall and then tie the walls together with rafters. Left as is, the post-and-beam framework can be used as an arbor or a trellis; roofed and sheathed with any of a variety of openwork materials *(pages 92-99)*, it becomes a breezy garden shelter. With weatherproof siding and roofing, the structure can be a shop, shed or studio.

The intended purpose determines the foundation of a post-and-beam building. For an open-roofed structure, a simple concrete slab or set of precast concrete piers is adequate *(pages 68-69)*. A closed-roofed structure, particularly one that must bear the weight of winter snows, should have a reinforced turned-down slab *(pages 106-111)* or concrete footings *(pages 54-56)*.

The size of the posts for an unroofed structure is determined by its width—the distance between the two walls. Long, narrow structures are easier to build, for if the width is less than 8 feet, 4-by-4 redwood or fir posts suffice. If the structure is wider than 8 feet but less than 12 feet, use 4-by-6 posts.

Determining the size of posts for a roofed post-and-beam structure requires more precise calculations. As a general rule, a roofed structure should be able to support a load of 50 pounds per square foot. To determine the size of post you will need, multiply the area of the structure by 50, then divide the answer by the number of posts you plan to put up. If the result is less than 8,000, use 4-by-4 posts, which can each support as much

as 8,000 pounds; if the figure is greater, use 4-by-6s, which can hold as much as 14,000 pounds each.

The size of the beams is determined by the span between posts. The width in inches of a 4-inch beam (sometimes referred to as a "4-by") should equal its span in feet. Thus, a 4-by-6 beam can span distances up to 6 feet, a 4-by-8 up to 8 feet, and so on.

Rafters to bridge the beams can be spaced as far apart as 48 inches in an unroofed structure; use the table below to determine the spacing and lengths of rafters for an open roof. If you plan to roof the structure, the rafters should be set no more than 16 inches apart. Use 2-by-4s for a structure up to 5 feet wide, 2-by-6s for up to 9 feet, 2-by-8s for up to 11 feet and 2-by-10s for up to 14 feet.

Rafter Sizes for an Open Roof

Spacing	Maximum rafter length		
	8 ft.	10 ft.	12 ft.
16 in.	2 × 4	2 × 6	2 × 6
32 in.	2 × 6	2 × 8	2 × 8
48 in.	2 × 6	2 × 8	2 × 10

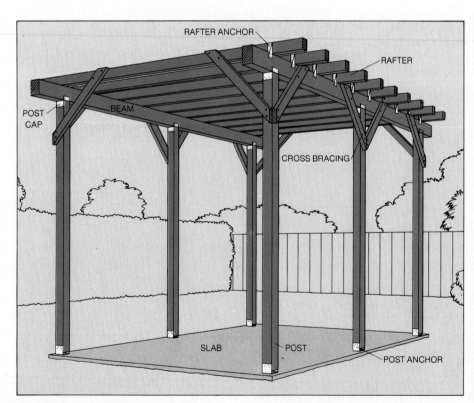

Anatomy of post-and-beam. Metal anchors hold together the basic post-and-beam framework. The posts are attached to post anchors fastened in a concrete slab, as above, or to precast concrete piers *(page 69)*. The post anchors are attached with lag bolts and lead shields.

At the tops of the posts, metal post caps secure the beams. Rafters are attached to beams with metal rafter anchors. The beam ends overhang the posts below them, and the rafters overhang the beams. Diagonal 2-by-4 cross bracing is lag-bolted to posts and beams.

Assembling the Structure

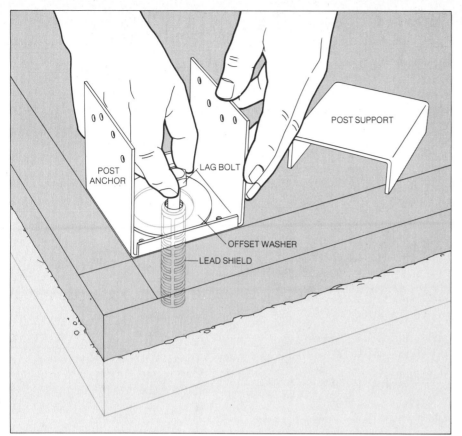

1 Setting the post anchors. The U-shaped anchors are bolted to the concrete slab or pier with an offset washer that permits post positions to be shifted for alignment. Place anchors and washers at each post position so that you can outline the washer holes, then drill a ¾-inch hole 4 inches deep at each mark and drop a ¾-inch lead shield into the hole. Replace the post anchor and washer over the hole and, with your fingers, screw a ½-inch lag bolt into the shield. Set a post support inside each anchor.

POST SUPPORT

POST ANCHOR

LAG BOLT

OFFSET WASHER

LEAD SHIELD

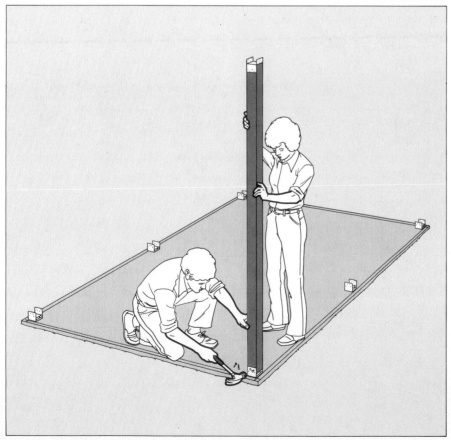

2 Raising the posts. Nail a post cap to the top of each post and, while a helper holds the post upright on its post support, nail the flanges of the post anchor to the bottom of the post. Use eightpenny galvanized nails.

3 **Plumbing and bracing the corners.** Attach 2-by-4 bracing to hold the corner posts plumb while a helper checks with a level. The top of the bracing must be at least 20 inches below the post tops. When corner posts are plumb, tighten the lag bolts under them (*inset*).

Mark the tops of the beams for rafters, spacing them as desired but making the first mark so as to position the outside edge of an end rafter flush with the outside edge of a corner post.

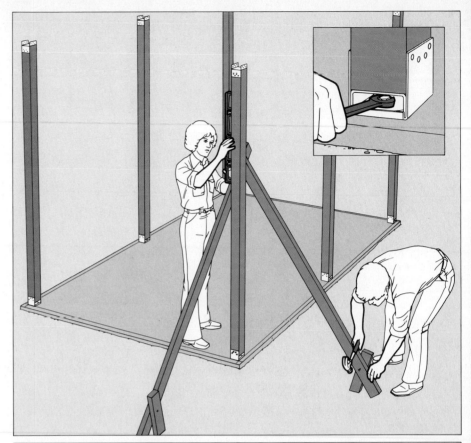

4 **Attaching the beams.** Set each beam atop a row of posts, marked side up, aligning the outermost marks with the outside edges of the end posts, and have a helper hold the beam steady while you nail the corner post-cap flanges to the beam. Plumb the inner posts with a level, nail them to the post-cap flanges, then tighten the lag bolts under the posts.

5 **Putting up rafters for an open roof.** Nail a rafter anchor on the top of one beam, to the right of an end-rafter mark. Nail another anchor on the top of the other beam, to the left of the mark. Mark the side of a rafter 12 inches in from each end, set it against the anchors and nail the rafter to the anchors with eightpenny nails. Similarly attach the remaining rafters.

Mark positions for the cross braces on the posts and beams. On the outside of each post except the end ones, set the mark at least 12½ inches from the top of the post. Mark the top of the beam at least 18 inches to the left and right of the center line of the post. On each end post, set the mark at least 18 inches down from the top of the beam, and mark the top of the beam at least 18 inches from the outside edge of the post. Cut 2-by-4 braces to fit the marks, angling the ends at a 45° angle.

6 **Mounting the braces.** Tack the braces in position, then secure them with ⅜-inch lag bolts 3 inches long, fitted with washers.

To make post-to-rafter braces at the ends of the structure, mark the end posts at least 12½ inches down from their tops and mark the tops of the end rafters at least 21½ inches in from the outer edge of each beam. Cut braces to fit, tack them in place and attach them to the posts with ⅜-inch lag bolts 3 inches long, and to the rafters with ⅜-inch lag bolts 2½ inches long. Remove the tacking and temporary bracing.

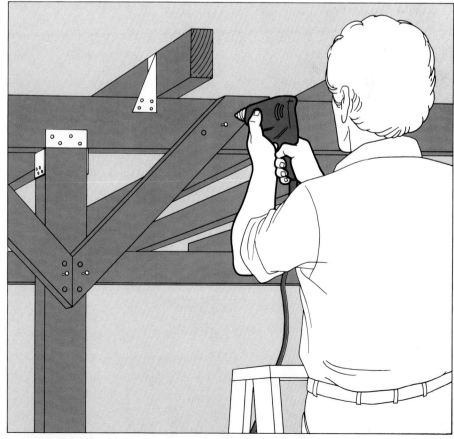

Installing Sloping Roofs

To provide a weathertight roof for an open beam structure, install sloping rather than horizontal rafters and cover them with sheathing and roofing material (pages 90-91). No special calculations are needed; simply estimate the length of the rafters after determining the desired pitch of the roof. This informal kind of carpentry is less precise than the techniques that building a dwelling demand but will serve admirably for a simple outdoor structure.

For a shed roof, build a post-and-beam structure with the posts higher on one side than on the other by an amount determined by the desired roof pitch; in the example at right, the rise is 1 inch for each foot of an 8-foot run—a difference in height of 8 inches.

A gable roof is a simple alternative and an appropriate covering for a post-and-beam structure like the one on page 74, which has sides of even height.

Marking rafters for a shed roof. Have a helper align a rafter board, on which a chalk line has been snapped down the middle, so that the top of the board touches the top of the higher crossbeam and the chalk line touches the top outer edge of the lower crossbeam. Tack the rafter to the upper crossbeam, and mark along the outside and top edges of the lower crossbeam for a bird's-mouth cut, a notch that fits the rafter snugly to the crossbeam. Then mark the rafter along the inner face of the upper crossbeam for the ridge cut, the cut that fits the rafter

to the upper crossbeam. Using a level, mark an overhang cut on the outward end of the rafter.

Using the marked rafter as a template, cut the remaining rafters. Toenail them on 16-inch centers to premarked spots on the upper crossbeam, and secure the bird's-mouth cut to the lower beam (inset) with metal rafter anchors. To brace the structure, lag-bolt 2-by-6 collar beams to each pair of end posts; toenail another collar beam between the center posts and reinforce it with 3-inch metal straps.

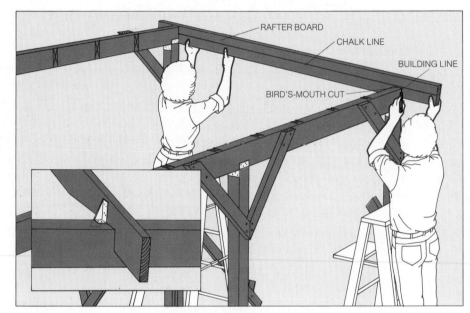

RAFTER BOARD
CHALK LINE
BUILDING LINE
BIRD'S-MOUTH CUT

Framing a Peaked Roof

1 **Marking rafters for a gable roof.** Have a helper align the rafter board to a crossbeam and a marking guide and, after tacking it to the marking guide, mark the bird's-mouth cut. To construct and place the marking guide, attach a scrap piece of wood the same thickness as the ridge beam and long enough to extend beyond the apex of the roof you envision, to a plank long enough to span the structure. Attach a diagonal brace to both the plank and the marking guide and position the plank on the crossbeams so that the marking guide is equidistant from them. Finally, tack the plank to both crossbeams. Mark the ridge cut and, using a carpenter's level, the overhang cut, and use this board as a template to cut the other rafters. Remove the plank and temporary marking guide.

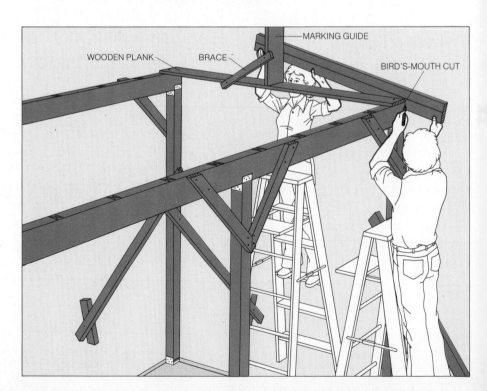

WOODEN PLANK
BRACE
MARKING GUIDE
BIRD'S-MOUTH CUT

2 **Assembling the frame.** On the ground, cut a 1-by-8 ridge beam to the same length as the crossbeams, mark it for rafters at 16-inch intervals and spike precut end rafters to one side of it with three 16-penny galvanized nails. Toe-nail the other end rafters to the opposite side of the beam. Brace the structure temporarily with 2-by-4s spiked across the opposite rafters.

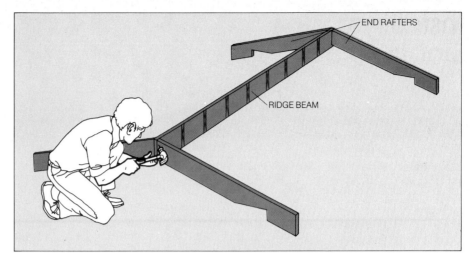

END RAFTERS

RIDGE BEAM

3 **Setting the frame in place.** With three helpers—two at the far end of the roof, one at your end—lift the frame into place, setting the bird's-mouth cuts of the rafters onto the crossbeams. If necessary, remove the temporary bracing so you can adjust the fit of the rafters, and replace it when they are correctly positioned. Spike the rafters to one side of the ridge beam and toenail them to the other side, using three 16-penny galvanized nails, then nail them to the rafter anchors *(page 78)*.

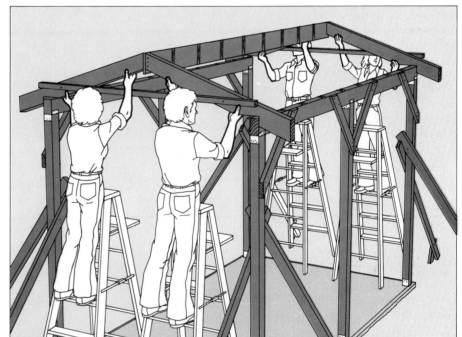

4 **Fitting the collar beams.** Set a 2-by-6 cut to the width of the structure atop the crossbeams and against a pair of end rafters, and mark it along the top of the rafters. Cut the board at the marks and use it as a template for the other collar beams. Nail collar beams to the end rafters with six eightpenny galvanized nails.

Mount the rest of the rafters, nailing a precut collar beam to each pair of rafters as you go; then remove the temporary bracing.

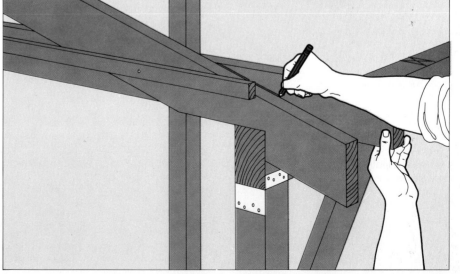

Gazebos: A Bit of Nostalgia

The gazebo—the word is redolent with antique charm—is an open post-and-beam structure usually of five, six or eight sides topped with a peaked roof. The Victorians, whose name for this airy summer house is mock-Latin for "I shall gaze," decorated their gazebos with everything from ornately carved scrollwork and wrought-iron ornaments to rustic twigs and branches with the bark left on.

The gazebo is still popular as a summer garden shelter, combining 19th Century charm with the openness and simplicity of more conventional post-and-beam structures. Once erected, the structure can be either left open or covered with woven reed or bamboo *(pages 97, 99)*, with plastic or aluminum screening *(pages 94-95, 99)* or with lattice *(pages 92-93)*, and it can be decorated with whatever curlicues the owner fancies.

A gazebo like the one at right, consisting of a six-sided wooden platform set on masonry blocks, avoids the necessity of casting a slab or setting posts in a perfect hexagon. If the site is uneven, embed the blocks in the earth to level their tops. The six supporting posts are attached to the platform, which is strong enough to bear their weight and that of the beam-and-rafter unit that forms the roof. Install handrails in all but the entryway section to give rigidity to the structure, and set a masonry block at the front of this open section to serve as a step.

First determine the length of the platform's sides. Measure the radius of however large a circle the platform will occupy. The sides of a hexagon whose points touch the circumference of that circle will be the same as the radius; for a pentagon, multiply the radius by 1.25; for an octagon, by .75.

Cut the perimeter boards to the proper length and miter their ends to an angle of 30° for a hexagon, 36° for a pentagon or 22½° for an octagon. Cut the spacers (the boards that separate the rafters) in the same way. Use a framing square to mark face cuts for the crossbeams and rafters. To assemble the roof, you will need to build a nailing platform. Finally, you may want to rent two scaffolds to use in lifting the roof into place.

Anatomy of a hexagonal gazebo. Six 4-by-4 posts toenailed to a wooden deck form the uprights of this post-and-beam structure. The gazebo deck, which simply rests on masonry blocks, consists of perimeter boards, floor joists and decking, all of 2-by-6s. Six horizontal crossbeams, a set of five handrails and a set of six plywood arches give the structure lateral rigidity. The roof rafters of the gazebo are nailed at their bases to the crossbeams and attached at their peaks to 2-by-4 spacers.

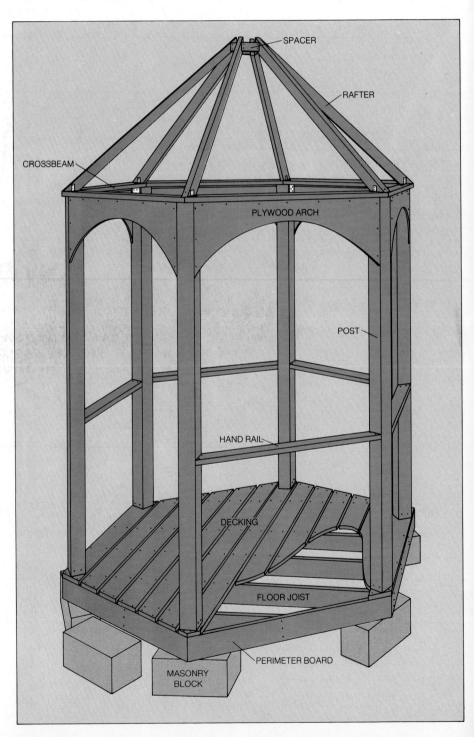

1 **Making the base.** After cutting both ends of six 2-by-6s with a circular saw set at a 30° angle, apply a liberal amount of exterior-grade carpenter's glue to the board ends and assemble the base. Nail two corrugated frame fasteners into the joints *(inset)*. Reinforce the inside joints of the assembled base with 3-inch metal truss plates that have been bent to fit the inside angle of the joints. Assemble the horizontal crossbeams for the roof of the gazebo by the same techniques, and cut the five lengths of 2-by-4 handrail.

2 **Putting in floor joists.** Nail 2-by-6 joists, aligned on 16-inch centers, to the gazebo base. Cut the joist ends at an angle, if necessary, to match the angle of the perimeter boards. Lay decking boards at right angles to the joists, and trim the deck edges with a circular saw *(page 101, Step 3)*. Place six masonry blocks on the ground or on a bed of gravel, to serve as supports for the gazebo base. Use a water level *(page 101)* to even the height of the blocks. Then position the completed base on blocks.

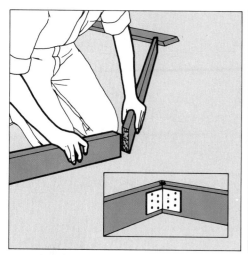

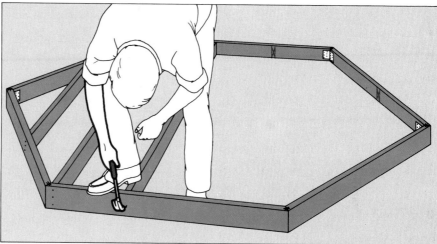

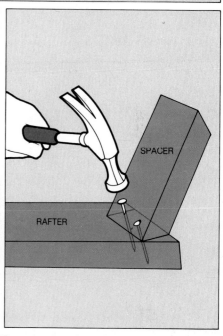

3 **Putting up the posts.** After cutting 4-by-4 posts to the desired height, toenail the first post to the deck with four 16-penny nails. Plumb and brace the post *(page 36)* and erect and secure the remaining ones, bracing each post to the adjacent one with temporary stiffeners *(overleaf)*.

4 **Preparing the rafters.** After cutting the rafter ends to match the desired pitch of the gazebo roof, cut six spacer boards to the desired length and toenail one to the peak end of each rafter while it rests on the ground.

Then position the base of the first rafter board over a joint of the crossbeam roof base, toenail the rafter in place with a 10-penny nail and secure the connection with 2-inch angle brackets.

5 **Assembling the roof frame.** Attach a second
rafter with its spacer as you did the first, then toenail the free end of the first spacer to the open
end of the second rafter. To facilitate nailing, slip
a temporary platform—built with 2 by 4s to
the exact height of the spacers above the crossbeams—underneath the spacers, and brace
the edge of the rafter with your leg. Add the remaining rafters and spacers the same way.

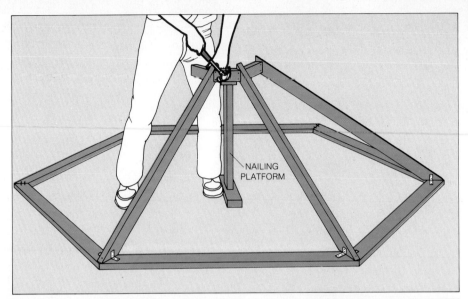

NAILING
PLATFORM

6 **Placing the roof.** Have two helpers hand the
roof up to you and a third helper standing at the
ends of two scaffolds, placed at opposite sides
of the gazebo. Carefully walk the roof into place;
position it with the outer edges of the crossbeams resting on the corners of the posts.

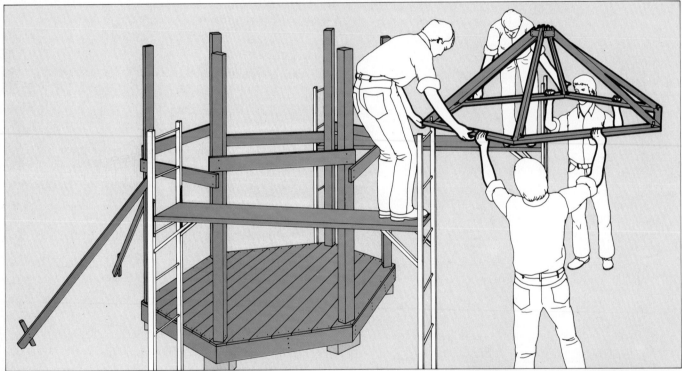

7 **Fastening the roof.** Drive a 16-penny nail
through the ends of all the crossbeams and into
the top of each post *(right)*. Then nail a 3-inch
metal angle plate to both sides of each post with
eightpenny nails *(far right)*.

Attach handrails to the posts with angle brackets. Fasten 1-by-1 nailing blocks to the underside
of the crossbeams and install plywood arches,
cut at a 30° angle to fit between posts.

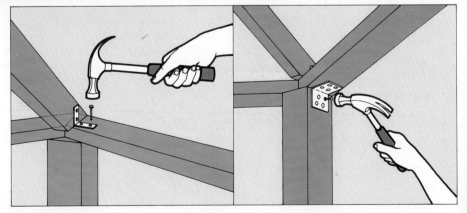

Tree Houses: Perches for Young Adventurers

Children love tree houses of all shapes and sizes, whether mere platforms or elaborate arboreal hideaways complete with doors, windows and pulleys to raise and lower picnic baskets.

Tree-house platforms may be attached to strong limbs of a low-branching tree, atop horizontal crossbeams. The design has to suit the tree—a tree with three main branches going off at angles is easiest to work with. Or, in the fashion of structures built around high-branching trees on the White House grounds by Presidents John F. Kennedy and Jimmy Carter, the tree-house platform can be set on freestanding posts.

Safety comes first in designing and building tree houses. Even the most carefully built ones are subject to unusual stress, and their height is a hazard. A tree house made for small children should be within 8 to 10 feet of the ground, and located within sight of the main dwelling. Guard rails at least 3 feet high around the sides of any elevated structure are a mandatory safety feature. As an added measure to cushion the shock of an accidental fall, rake the ground beneath the structure free of rocks, then line it with two or three inches of sawdust, tanbark or pine needles.

When attaching a platform frame to a tree, inspect all the branches that you will nail into, to make sure that the tree wood is free from rot, and later check periodically to make sure that high winds or tree growth have not weakened a supporting brace of the platform. Apply tree-wound paint wherever you cut away branches. Do not skimp on nailing; the nails will not hurt the tree if you spread tree-wound paint around them.

A structure nailed to branches. A typical tree-house platform, attached to a tree that has strong, spreading limbs, rests on 2-by-6 cross-beams nailed between the branches and is braced with 2-by-4s attached to the tree and to the platform frame. The base of the tree house is a framed deck of 1-by-6s laid atop 2-by-6 joists. When building the base, leave one of the end decking boards out so the platform can be hoisted into the tree (*page 84, Step 2*). Guard rails and garden fencing add security.

A small roofed structure sheathed with plywood occupies part of the deck, while a ladder (or a series of cleats nailed to the tree trunk) gives access to a trap door cut in the platform.

JOIST

CROSSBEAM

BRACE

Hoisting and Securing the Platform

1 **Installing crossbeams.** Select a site for the platform. With a helper, nail two or three 2-by-6 horizontal crossbeams to the tree at the same height and level. Measure carefully the space the platform will occupy on the crossbeams.

2 **Raising the platform.** Loop a length of nylon rope around one frame member and use a pulley to hoist the platform up to the crossbeams. With assistance from two helpers on ladders, set the platform onto the crossbeams.

3 Bracing the platform. Working from a ladder with its top rungs resting evenly on a scrap 2-by-4 nailed to a branch, nail at least three diagonal 2-by-4 braces between the underside of the platform and the tree. To provide reasonably good nailing surfaces for the braces, you may have to trim the ends of the 2-by-4s somewhat until you achieve an appropriate fit. Or you may have to nail a cleat to the tree or the platform and attach the end of the brace to the cleat.

A Deck Built around a Tree

A freestanding platform. For trees with high-branching trunks, build an elevated deck, supported by 4-by-4 posts anchored to concrete piers. Make the platform as for the post-and-beam floor *(pages 100-101)* and nail headers around the gap in the frame where the tree trunk will be. Attach diagonal braces from the posts to the frame with lag screws. Then nail 1-by-6 flooring boards directly to the joists, leaving a small gap around the tree trunk. Make a guardrail of 2-by-4s and enclose the open space between the rail and the deck with wood or metal fencing.

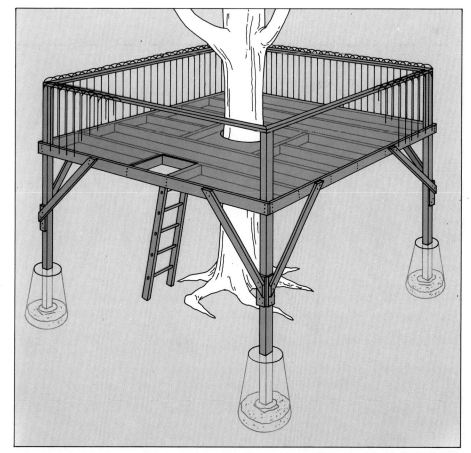

The Dome: A Sturdy Bubble of Wooden Triangles

The geodesic dome, invented by Buckminster Fuller in 1951, ingeniously combines equal-sided isosceles triangles into a pattern of hexagons and pentagons to form a hemisphere that is larger and stronger than any conventional structure that can be built with the same quantity of identical materials.

A dome like the one shown on the following pages, easily built of 1-by-1 wooden struts stapled together, is cheap, strong, attractive and versatile. It can span up to 30 feet without internal bracing, making it ideal for almost any backyard shelter calling for light, airy, uninterrupted interior space. It makes a fine cover for a swimming pool to keep out airborne debris and to warm the water by trapping solar heat. A door or window can be created simply by hinging one of the dome's triangles *(page 89)*; to keep the structure strong, never hinge two adjacent triangles.

This particular dome is a fair-weather structure, difficult to leakproof but easy to disassemble for off-season storage. Building it involves three simple, repetitive operations: cutting the struts, assembling them into triangles and attaching the triangles to one another. Cutting the struts to the right length is a matter of applying the table at right; mitering strut ends to the correct angles is easy to do with a homemade jig *(right)*.

The angles given for the strut ends will result in triangles with slight gaps at the corners opening to the inside of the triangle frame. This assures that the tips of the struts will meet and the outside dimensions of the triangles will be exact.

Before assembling the dome, prepare its cover by wrapping each triangle with a flexible covering or attaching a triangular piece of plywood or solid plastic. Use flexible, ultraviolet-resistant plastic on light-trapping domes for pools and gardens, colored plastic for a shade house. Plastic screening keeps bugs out and wire mesh keeps birds out—or in.

Plastic-sheathed domes can be partly weatherproofed by sealing all joints with plastic tape, but will still leak around windows and doors. As plastic or other covering deteriorates, replace it by removing and recovering affected frames.

In windy locations, cut 3-inch hardboard reinforcement disks with a hole saw and screw them to the struts where the points of triangles meet, using one 1-inch wood screw per strut.

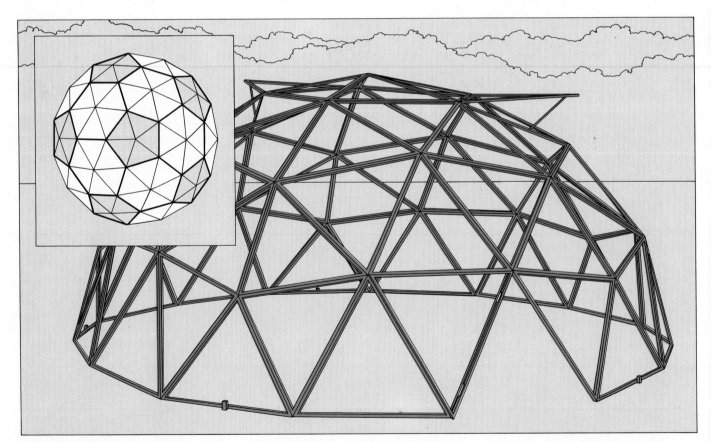

A homemade hemisphere. The dome shown here is composed of two sizes of triangular wooden frames made from straight, knot-free 1-by-1s. It is covered with clear plastic and has hinged vents and a door opening. Seen from above *(inset)*, the dome is a pattern of pentagons formed from short triangles (gray), and hexagons formed from tall triangles (white). Each kind of triangle has two legs of equal length and a base of a different length. The bases are the heavy lines of the inset; the legs converge at the centers of the hexagons and pentagons. The lengths of the legs and bases vary with the size of the dome but the angles at which they meet *(Step 1, opposite)* are always the same.

Finding the Lengths of Struts for a Dome

Diameter of dome	Height	Tall triangle struts		Short triangle struts	
		base	leg	base	leg
10 ft.	4 ft.	24¼ in.	24¾ in.	24¼ in.	20⅞ in.
15 ft.	6 ft.	36⅜ in.	37½ in.	36⅜ in.	31⅜ in.
20 ft.	8 ft.	48⅜ in.	49½ in.	48⅜ in.	41⅞ in.
25 ft.	10 ft.	60½ in.	61¾ in.	60½ in.	52¼ in.
30 ft.	12 ft.	72⅝ in.	74¼ in.	72⅝ in.	62¾ in.

Domes cut to order. Make a dome in any of five sizes by cutting the struts to the lengths indicated in the table at left. Read down the left side of the table to find the diameter and height of the dome you want to make; read across to find the length of each strut from tip to tip of the mitered ends. Make 30 bases for short triangles and 60 legs; make 45 bases for tall triangles and 90 legs.

Cutting and Assembling the Framework

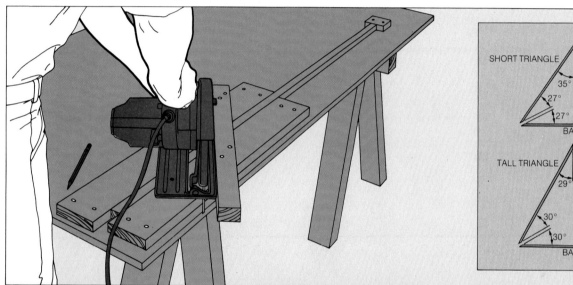

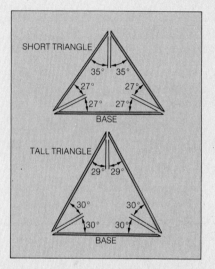

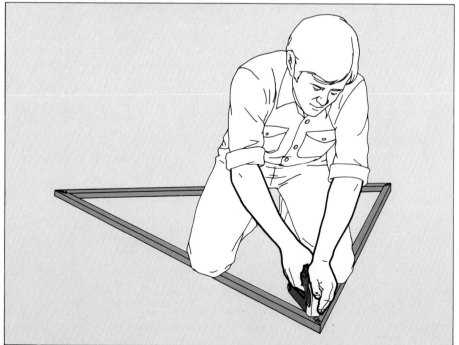

1 A jig for struts. Miter 1-by-1 lumber to the angles indicated in the inset above and to the lengths determined by the table (above, top) with a radial arm saw, a table saw or with a circular saw used in the homemade jig shown above at left. To make the jig, bracket a 1-by-1 with 1-by-4s nailed on a sheet of plywood; remove the 1-by-1. Nail a 1-by-2 fence across the 1-by-4s at the angle of the first cut you will make. Guide the saw along the fence to cut a kerf through the 1-by-4s, then measure back from the kerf to position a stopblock. Saw all the struts that require cuts at that angle, then move the fence, cut a new kerf and reset the stopblock as needed for other struts. Mark the strut ends with their angles.

2 Assembling the triangles. To form each of the 30 short and 45 tall triangles required, lay out three struts as shown above, hold two tips together and drive three staples across the joint with a heavy-duty staple gun. Similarly fasten the third strut, then turn the triangle over and triple-staple each joint from the other side. Paint the triangles.

3 **Covering the triangles.** Lay a triangle on a sheet of plastic, fold the plastic up over one strut and staple it near a corner. Stretch the plastic slightly along the strut to a second corner and staple it. Repeat for the other two struts; avoid leaving wrinkles at the corners. Then gently stretch the plastic and staple it to the rest of each strut, starting at the middle and working to the ends. Trim off excess plastic.

To cover a triangle with thin plywood or other solid material, lay the triangle on the material and trace around the edge. Cut the material along the traced lines and fasten it to the triangle with weatherproof staples, nails or screws.

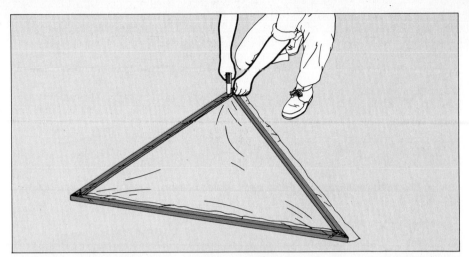

4 **Assembling the first course.** At a level site, hold two tall triangles edge to edge with their bases oriented as shown. Align the corners and staple the two inside edges together every 4 to 6 inches. Attach a third tall triangle to the right side of the second, oriented as shown in the inset. Continuing to the right, similarly attach three short triangles with the bases oriented as indicated in the inset. While helpers hold the triangles upright, add four more sets of tall and short triangles to the first set to form a circular fence leaning inward, with its plastic-covered side outward; staple the last triangle to the first.

Measure along the ground from the middle of the base of a short triangle to the point opposite it where the corners of three tall triangles meet near ground level. Make similar measurements in different directions and adjust the assembly of triangles to make all the measurements equal.

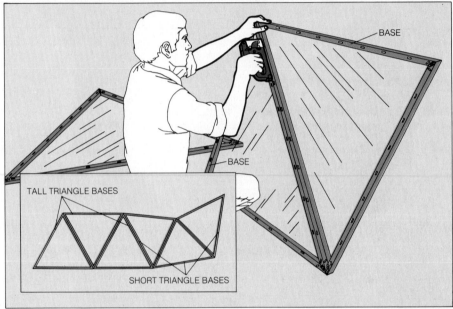

BASE

BASE

TALL TRIANGLE BASES

SHORT TRIANGLE BASES

5 **Staking down the dome.** Drive a 2-foot-long 2-by-2 wooden stake treated with a preservative into the ground alongside the middle of the base strut of a short triangle—one of the five points at which the dome's base sits firmly on the ground. Secure the stake to the strut with a 3-inch wood screw. Similarly stake down the base struts of the other four short triangles.

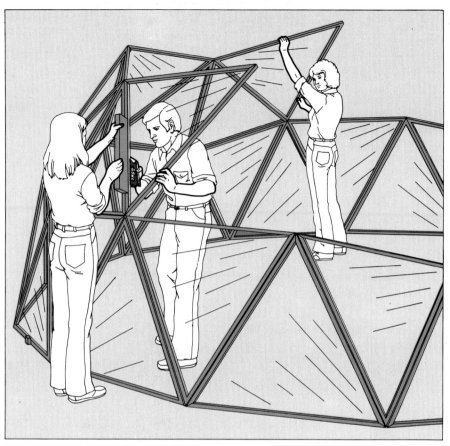

6 Finishing the dome. Following the pattern in the inset on page 86, install additional courses of triangles. Use a helper to hand in triangles, to help position them and to hold a block of wood opposite the staple gun to assure that the staples penetrate well. Have two others help keep the sides of the dome upright until you have completed the second course. When the sides of the dome rise too high to pass triangles over, make an opening in the dome by removing a tall base-down triangle from the first course. Installing the last few triangles may require you and your helper to stand on stepladders. If the last pair of triangles does not fit, release the dome from the stakes to fit the triangles in.

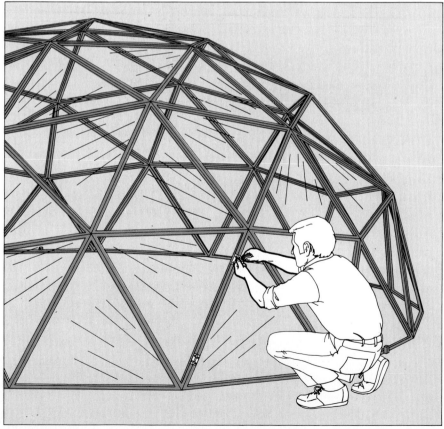

7 Making a door. Reattach with hinges the tall triangle you removed during construction. Reinforce with vinyl tape the opening edges of the door and the edges of the adjacent triangles that form the unhinged side of the doorjamb. Screw strips of wood to the jamb to form a doorstop. Latch the door with hooks and eyes.

Similarly make hinged windows. Alternatively, door and window openings can be made simply by removing individual frames.

A Wide Choice of Coverings for Top and Sides

You can enclose an outdoor structure the same way you would a house—add plywood or fiber sheathing plus shingles or clapboard and a built-up floor—and you should use such durable materials if the purpose of the building demands it. That is seldom the case, and lightweight coverings—often more attractive and functional than the standard ones—generally suffice for auxiliary buildings. To a great extent, the coverings depend on the construction method: for an A-frame, the roof is also the side walls; for a simple dome, very light covering supplies the roof and the walls.

While a rainproof roof is necessary for a storage shed, it can generally be made of corrugated plastic panels or plywood covered with inexpensive, quickly applied roll roofing. Many other structures—lawn pavilions, shade houses and the like—are more pleasant with open roofs. Open rafters, with decorative end cuts, may be enough alone or they can be joined by crosspieces. For more shade, you can cover the rafters with latticework or rows of slats or use some more exotic material such as shade cloth or woven reed or bamboo. You can use many of the same materials—lattice, bamboo or woven reed—as siding, or you can fill the open walls with aluminum or fiberglass screening to let in light and air while excluding bugs.

A floor often can be dispensed with, particularly for storage sheds on dry sites. You can use the ground as it is, cover it with gravel or sand, or pour a lightweight concrete slab. A slab will also serve as flooring for a pavilion or a shade house, but wood decking is generally more comfortable. Unless the structure is going to be fairly weathertight, such wood floors are generally made slatted to provide spaces for drainage *(pages 100-101)*.

Custom Cuts for Rafters

Designs for rafter ends. These six patterns are the most popular for adding a decorative touch to the plain ends of open-structure rafters. Enlarge the pattern you plan to use on graph paper and transfer it to a rafter. Use a saber saw with a rough-cut blade for the cuts.

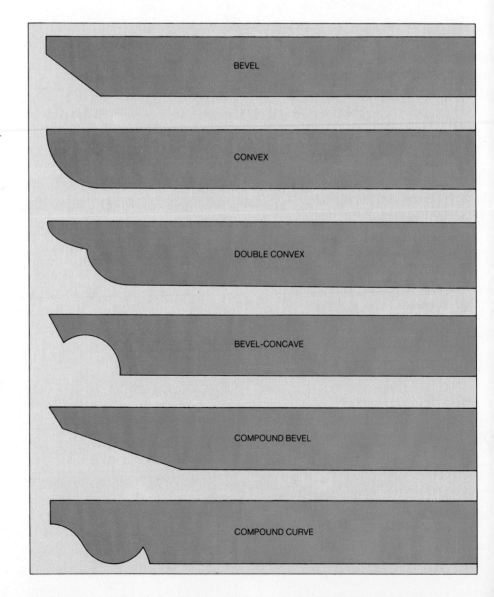

BEVEL

CONVEX

DOUBLE CONVEX

BEVEL-CONCAVE

COMPOUND BEVEL

COMPOUND CURVE

Simple Roofing that is Weatherproof

1 **Setting roll roofing.** Apply a plywood sheath and nail or staple the upper edge of a full-width strip of roll roofing so that it overlaps the eave, then fold it back so you can spread 12-inch-wide borders of cement on the sheathing. Press the strip firmly in place and nail its corners down.

Apply additional strips of roll roofing in the same way, allowing a 4-inch overlap of each upper strip over the strip below, until the roof is covered.

2 **Setting ridge pieces.** On a gable roof, cut pieces of roll roofing 12 inches by 36 inches and cement them along the ridge, overlapping 6 inches like shingles. Nail the last 6 inches of each piece to the roof, so that cement and the succeeding piece cover the nailheads.

On a shed roof, let the top strip overlap the upper edge of the plywood sheath 5 inches. Fold the overlap around the sheath edge and nail or staple it to the face of the upper crossbeam.

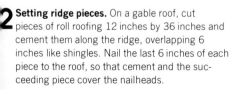

Openwork Roofs
for Light Shade

Slats for shades. Nail parallel rows of 1-by-2s to rafters, using a slat as a spacer and working down if the roof is pitched. To make a safe working platform on the roof, temporarily nail to the rafters a sheet of plywood with a 2-by-4 footstop along the lower edge. Move the platform as you work down the roof; near the eaves, finish the job from a ladder.

Staggered eggcrate crosspieces. For a distinctive open overhead pattern, mark for crosspieces between horizontal rafters, using a tape measure and combination square. Cut the crosspieces from boards of the same dimensions as the rafters and face-nail through the rafters into the end grain of the crosspieces.

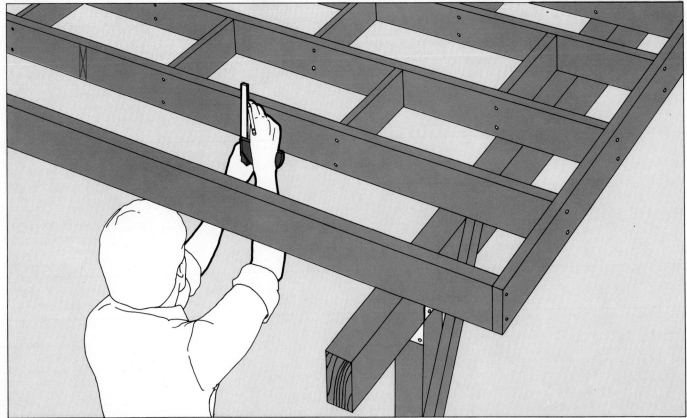

Installing Latticework

1 Laying out the lattice. Cut pieces of lath to approximate lengths for a crisscross pattern, then staple them at a 45° angle to the sides of a rectangular frame of 1-by-1s, using a length of lath as a spacer. Cut off the protruding ends of the lath evenly with a saber saw.

2 Attaching the frame. Using finishing nails, secure the lattice frame against 1-by-1 or 1-by-2 stops nailed along the inside edges of the structure's framework. Use a lightweight finishing hammer for greater accuracy.

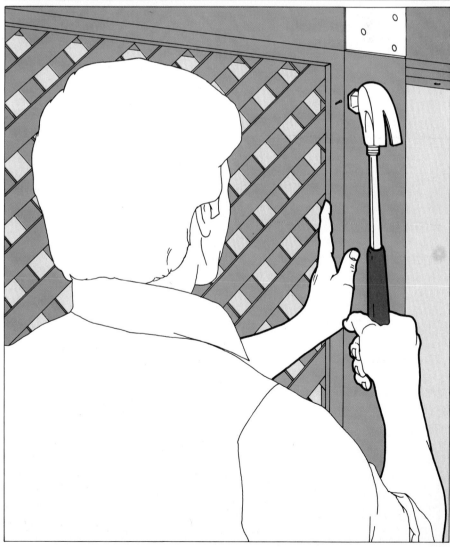

Making and Repairing Screens

Covering the sides or even the roof of an outdoor structure with screening makes an attractive compromise between openness to and protection from the outdoors. The screens allow air to circulate but keep insects out and, to some extent, soften the glare of sunlight. Moreover, they are simple and inexpensive to assemble and they give good service for years without maintenance.

Most screening is either aluminum or fiberglass. Aluminum screening corrodes in salt air, but resists tearing better than fiberglass and is easier to pull taut. Both materials come in packaged rolls in widths up to 48 inches and lengths up to 72 inches. Longer pieces will be cut to order by most building-supply dealers. The easiest—and generally the best—way to attach screening is to staple it directly to the wooden members of a wall or roof. Staple every 2 inches at one end, and then have an assistant draw the opposite end taut while you finish stapling. Follow the same procedure on the other two ends and nail molding over the edges of the screening to cover the staples.

Many people prefer, however, to put the screening on separate frames that can be attached to and removed from the structure like window screens. The frames can be made of wood—rectangles of 1-by-4s to which the screening is stapled—but aluminum frames, constructed from special channeling and connections, are easier to build.

Sections of aluminum screen frame, designed to be cut to size and snapped together over right-angle fasteners, are available at hardware stores in lengths up to 8 feet. They generally come with a spline—a length of rubber or vinyl tubing that clamps the screening inside a groove along the edges of a frame. To set the spline into the frame, you will need a screen-spline roller *(opposite, top)*, available from screening suppliers. The maximum size for a screening frame, whether wood or metal, is 4 feet by 8 feet. To screen larger areas, build several frames.

Small holes in any screening material can be patched by gluing a larger piece of the same material over the hole, but each material also has a special repair method. A fiberglass patch can be fused to the screening around the hole with an electric iron *(opposite, bottom);* for small holes in aluminum screening, you can either glue on cut-to-size patches or buy special screening patches with tiny hooks that lock into the screening. But larger holes or rips near the edge of a frame cannot be repaired effectively; you must replace the screening entirely.

A Detachable Screen Frame

1 **Assembling a metal frame.** Miter the ends of frame sections at a 45° angle with a hacksaw, keeping the spline groove toward the inside of the frame; then slip adjoining ends over a right-angle metal fastener to lock each corner.

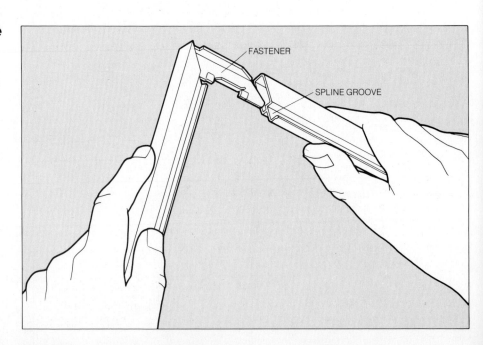

FASTENER

SPLINE GROOVE

2 Inserting the screening. Cut screening slightly larger than the frame, snipping off corners at 45° to prevent bunching, and secure the screening to one side of the frame with C clamps. Then pull the screening taut to the opposite side and roll the concave wheel of a screen-spline roller over a length of spline to sandwich the edge of the screening into the frame groove. Release the clamps, sandwich the first side in place, and repeat the procedure on the other two sides of the frame. Trim off excess screening.

When working with either metal or stiff plastic screening, you may have to crease the screening into the frame groove with the convex wheel of the roller before installing the spline.

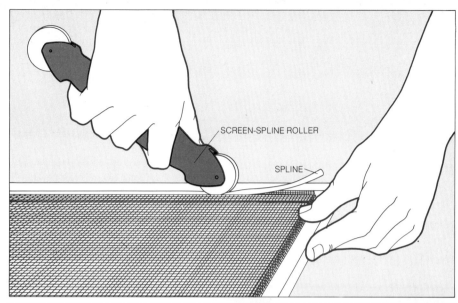

3 Hanging the screen. To fit a metal frame into a large rectangular opening, slip its top into a ½-inch aluminum U channel screwed into the top of the opening. Nail shoe molding along the opening's sides and bottom; this will act as a stop to keep the screen frame in place. Install the U channel and molding near the inside or outside edge of the frame, depending on whether you want the screen to mount from the inside or the outside of the structure. To lock the frame use turn buttons, screwed into the bottom and side edges of the structure (inset).

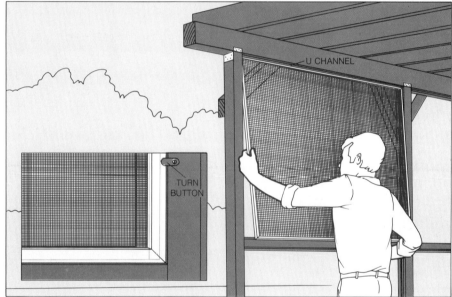

Patching Small Holes in Fiberglass Screening

A simple hot patch. Lay the screen flat on an ironing board and cover the hole with a patch an inch larger on all sides than the opening. Cover the patch with a thin cotton rag and run the edge of an electric iron at its hottest setting slowly over the outside edges of the patch until the patch fuses to the screening.

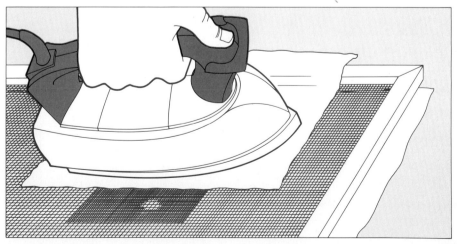

Airy Sheathing, Easy to Mount

You can use any of a number of lightweight and inexpensive materials to add the siding and roofing to outdoor structures that you plan to use only in warm weather. Exotic materials—bamboo, woven reed or synthetics, shade cloth or corrugated plastic—are especially suitable for structures like domes, trellises or tree houses because they require minimal support and can be quickly attached to almost any existing framework.

Woven reed, bamboo and shade cloth protect from the sun but only corrugated plastic will keep off heavy rain. If the structure will shelter shade-loving plants, you may wish to use shade cloth, which is available in a variety of weaves that admit different amounts of light. Woven reed and bamboo are normally used to cover outdoor living spaces.

Of these materials, the easiest to install is shade cloth made of synthetic fiber; the polypropylene is preferred by many for its durability and light weight. Shade cloth must be specially ordered through a nursery or garden shop, which will cut it to size, reinforce the sides and install grommets to your specifications. Order shade cloth cut 4 inches smaller all around than your roof so you can lace it in place (below). Specify reinforced edges and No. 2 brass grommets, one in each corner, two 3 inches from each cor-

ner and the rest spaced 18 inches apart.

Untreated bamboo and woven reed are cheaper and more natural-looking than shade cloth and, because they can be trimmed to size with metal shears, do not have to be specially ordered. The bamboo shades sold for use on windows can be applied to side openings.

Woven reed, also used for both siding and roofing, is sold in 6-foot-wide rolls in 15- to 25-foot lengths. For a roof, the reed can be sandwiched between 1-by-1s and galvanized wire. For siding, it can be stapled to removable 2-by-2 frames.

Corrugated plastic panels, reinforced with fiberglass, are more difficult to install—they need to be nailed to special filler strips (pages 98-99)—but they provide rain protection. They should be installed on a roof with a minimum pitch of 1 inch to 1 foot or, in a snowfall area, a pitch of at least 3 inches to 1 foot.

Plastic panels come in standardized widths that work with rafters spaced 16 or 24 inches apart. Most building-supply companies carry these sheets in 8- to 12-foot lengths, and longer lengths can be specially ordered. They can be cut to size with a fine-toothed handsaw or a circular saw fitted with an abrasive blade. Install the sheets in courses, starting at the low edge of the roof, and overlap courses to make the roof watertight.

Using Shade Cloth and Woven Reed

Attaching shade cloth. To lace shade cloth to a roof, install 3¾-inch lag bolts in the corners, stretch the precut fabric across the roof and tie the corner grommets to the eyebolts, using a double square knot. Screw additional eyebolts along the sides of the roof, lining them up opposite the grommets in the cloth.

Tie one end of a length of synthetic cord to a corner eyebolt and lace the free end of the cord through the corner grommet to the next eyebolt, from there to the adjacent grommet and so on to the end of the side. Similarly lace the opposite side. With a helper, hand-tighten the lacing on both sides, keeping the fabric centered between the exterior rafters. Similarly lace and hand-tighten the two remaining sides.

EYEBOLTS

GROMMETS

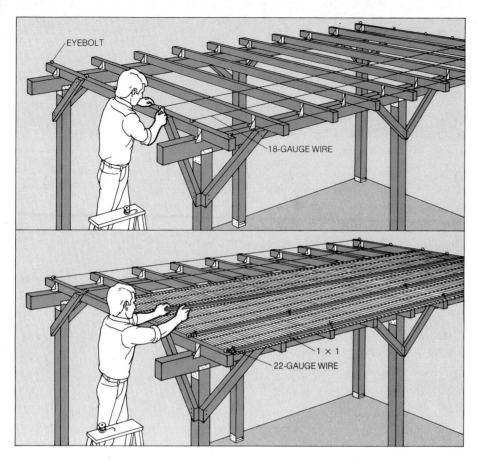

Roofing with woven reed. After installing 3¾-inch eyebolts every 22 inches along the tops of the end rafters, stretch galvanized 18-gauge wires across the roof and tie them to opposite eyebolts *(left, above)*. Place the woven reed on top of the wires and lay 1-by-1s on top of the reed.

Fasten the 1-by-1s every 4 feet with lengths of 22-gauge wire threaded through the reeds and around the 18-gauge wire, and secured with a twist at the top of the 1-by-1s *(left, below)*.

Techniques for Reed and Bamboo

Siding with woven reed. Tack 2-by-2s flush with the support posts *(far left)*: the corner 2-by-2s flush with the outside of the building *(inset)*, the center 2-by-2s flush with the edges of the support posts. If necessary, remove the angle braces. Screw metal plates at the top, center and bottom of each 2-by-2. Cut three 2-by-2s to fit between each set of vertical 2-by-2s. Place them horizontally between the metal plates and screw them in position. Screw the vertical 2-by-2s to the support and corner posts with flathead wood screws, two to a post.

Cut the woven reed flush with the outer edges of the frame. With a helper holding the reed, staple the top corner to the frame with 1-inch galvanized staples *(left)*, then staple it every 6 inches along the top, sides and bottom.

Hanging bamboo shades. With the shade on a flat surface, tie the cord furnished with the shade to the back of the single pulley *(below, left)*, run it down the back of the shade, up the front and through the first pulley *(below, center)*. Then run the cord across and through the double pulley and form a loop *(below, right)*.

Pull the remaining length of cord down the front of the shade and up the back and tie it to the back of the double pulley.

Roll the blinds up and mark the position of the eye hooks against the beam. Predrill holes and screw the hooks in, using pliers for leverage.

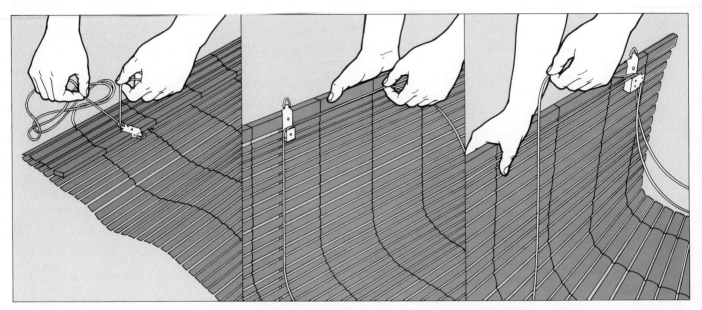

A Translucent, Rainproof Roof

1 Attaching the filler strips. After installing a fascia board and nailing cross supports between the rafters at 3-foot intervals, nail the scalloped wooden filler strips along the tops of the fascia board and on top of the cross supports. Then cut and fasten the plain wooden strips to the tops of all but the end rafters.

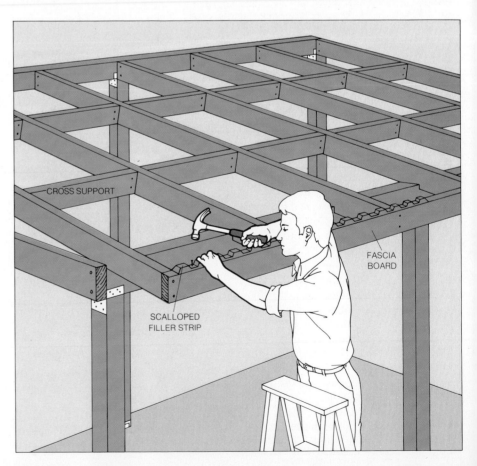

CROSS SUPPORT

FASCIA BOARD

SCALLOPED FILLER STRIP

2 **Installing the panels.** Beginning at the lowest point on the slope of the roof, lay the first sheet over the rafters so that the last valley of the corrugated plastic sheet lies flat against the end rafter. Caution: in high-wind areas, always lay the first panel farthest from the direction of the prevailing wind. Drill holes slightly smaller than your nails through the valley of the plastic on the end rafters, through every second ridge along the fascia and the cross supports, and along the rafters every 12 to 15 inches. Secure the plastic with self-sealing roofing nails.

Overlap the panels on the rafters, sealing the joints with nonsetting mastic to the lower panel *(inset)*. Predrill and nail the panels together.

If you are sheathing a gable-roofed structure, the ridge edge of the panels should be secured after you have installed the aluminum ridge-roll flashing supplied by the manufacturer.

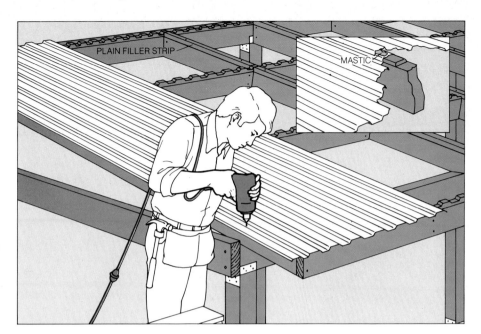

PLAIN FILLER STRIP

MASTIC

A Tropical Topping of Split Bamboo

With a few simple hand tools, you can build a pavilion of bamboo, much like the one that so impressed Marco Polo as he arrived in the city of Shandu. The building shown here, while it lacks the gilt and the silken walls of the Oriental palace, is an attractive and functional structure based on modern structural techniques and ancient craftsmanship.

After the gable roof is built *(pages 78-79)*, a layer of 3-inch split bamboo poles spaced an inch apart is laid, round side down, between the ridge and beams and attached with thin galvanized wires or with common nails. Then another layer of split bamboo is placed over the first layer, round side up, to form a durable, watertight roof. The bottom layer acts as a rain gutter; the overlapping second layer seals the joints. A last overlapping layer of bamboo is laid at the peak to form a ridge cap.

A "poor man's timber" in the tropics, bamboo is hard to find in northern climates. If used, it should be treated with a heavy coat of marine varnish to protect it from rot. Because of its high tensile strength, bamboo can be used over very widely spaced rafters, but if you need to nail it to supports between rafters, predrill nail holes in the bamboo to prevent it from splitting.

Wooden Floors for Comfort

Floors are an integral part of some structures: the A-frame, gazebo and tree house all depend on their floors for support. Other buildings, which rest on belowground footings or a concrete slab, as does the post-and-beam structure at right, are built without floors and may not need any. But to provide a dry and ventilated surface to walk on or to serve as a platform for storage, an additional wooden floor may be desirable. For a permanent deck, build an understructure as shown at top right. For a removable floor, build portable deck modules, called duckboards, to rest on the ground or slab (*opposite, bottom*).

The deck surface can be 2-by-2s, 2-by-4s or 2-by-6s spaced ¼ inch apart for good drainage. Laid flat, these boards are normally nailed to 2-by-6 or 2-by-8 joists spaced 16 inches on center.

Wherever possible, lay the boards so that the rings visible in the end grain are crest up: if the board warps, it will bend along the lines of the rings and shed water easily. And you can avoid splitting the board ends when nailing by first blunting the nail points with a hammer.

Adding a Permanent Deck

1 Building the understructure for a deck. Attach 2-by-8s with lag screws to the outsides of the posts, then nail joist hangers inside this frame for 2-by-8 interior joists spaced 16 inches apart. After you have installed the joists, nail 2-by-8 bridging boards between them in a staggered pattern. Finally, attach nailing cleats to the posts of the structure at the height of the joists to provide support for the deck boards whose ends will butt the posts.

2 Fastening the boards. Nail several feet of decking, with the boards spaced ¼ inch apart. As you proceed, use a tape measure to be sure that the boards are not drifting out of parallel with the understructure. If you find a deviation, correct it by adjusting the angle of the next few boards. Caution: make these angle adjustments well within the floor area; the final decking board must align with the end of the understructure precisely.

3 Squaring the end boards. It is generally easier to lay the boards of a deck without trying to line up edges exactly—the lengths of pieces vary a bit—then square off all the ends at once with a circular saw. Trim one board to the overhang you prefer—up to 2 inches is usual—then nail a lath strip to the deck boards as a cutting jig so that the left edge of the saw's horizontal platform, or shoe, guides the blade.

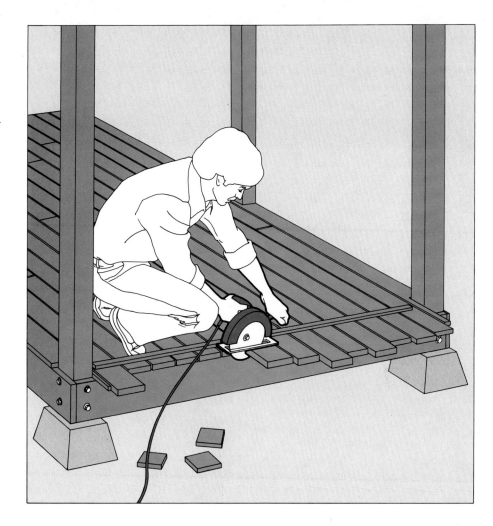

Putting Together a Portable Platform

Making duckboard decking. Face-nail 2-by-6 boards onto a 3- or 4-foot square understructure, made by butt-nailing pressure-treated 2-by-4s. Space the boards about ¼ inch apart, using a strip of plywood as a guide, but adjust spacing of the last few boards so that the outermost board fits the end of the frame precisely.

Make as many of these miniature decks as you need to cover the floor, adjusting size so they fit.

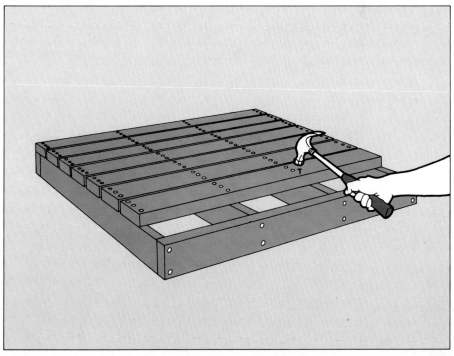

A Glassed-in Framework to Nurture Seedlings

A cold frame looks like a low box set flat in the ground. It is in fact a miniature greenhouse with a hinged glass or plastic roof. Within the frame, soil and air are warmed by the sun's rays even while the temperature outdoors is below freezing, and you can start seedlings long before the beginning of the growing season. When spring comes, you can replant the seedlings elsewhere in the garden and enjoy flowers, fruits and vegetables far sooner than unaided nature would allow.

For the cold frame's top, or sash, you can use an old storm window. Make the walls of rot-resistant cedar, redwood or cypress (or less expensive wood treated with preservative), matching their dimensions to the size of the sash—typically 2½ feet by 4 feet. For larger cold frames, use two or more windows, mounted side by side. If you do not have a spare storm window and cannot buy an old one at a reasonable cost, build a frame of 2-by-2s and cover each face of the frame with a sheet of plastic. Air trapped between the two sheets of plastic provides insulation for the cold frame.

Slope the side walls of the frame from a height of 12 inches in back to 6 inches in front, and set it facing south, so that the roof slants toward the noon sun. Treat all wooden parts that are not naturally rot-resistant with copper naphthenate, a preservative that does not harm plants; do not use creosote, pentachlorophenol or mercury compounds to preserve the wood—they are toxic to plants. Paint the inside of the frame white so it will reflect the sun's light and heat.

Finally, install a prop to hold the sash open for cooling—a temperature above 70° inside the frame could injure the seedlings. The design shown will hold the sash securely even on windy days. To stop excess heat loss on frosty nights, drape a tarpaulin over the cold frame or pile leaves or straw around it.

You can, if you like, warm the plants with a heating cable and thermostat, available from gardening stores, to convert your cold frame to a hotbed. Dig out the soil inside the frame to a depth of 6 inches, put in a 2-inch layer of sand and zigzag the heating cable on the sand. To protect the cable from damage, cover it with ½-inch screen mesh, then cover the screen with 4 to 6 inches of soil.

1 **Making the side walls.** Lay a window sash atop a length of 2-by-12, with one corner touching a line marked 5¼ inches above the lower edge of the board and the other protruding ¼ inch beyond an upper corner. Mark the diagonal and cut along it to make one frame side, then use the cut board as a template to cut the other side. For the back and front of the frame, cut a 2-by-12 board and a 2-by-6 board to match the length of the window sash less 3 inches.

2 Assembling the frame. Screw the side boards to the front and back pieces, plane the top edges of the front and back to match the side slope, and anchor the frame in the ground. Dig a 2-inch trench in the soil, sink the frame in place, then drive 2-by-2 stakes at the inside corners, using 18-inch stakes at the back and 12-inch stakes at the front. Attach the frame to the stakes with wood screws. Use butt hinges to attach the window to the back of the frame.

3 Rigging the prop sticks. Glue four ½-inch dowels into holes bored toward the front of the frame and sash sides *(below, top)*, using dowels 5 inches long in the frame and 4 inches long in the sash. Drill ⅛-inch holes through the dowels. Make two prop sticks from 24-inch lengths of 1-by-2, drilled with ⅝-inch holes at 2-inch intervals. Slip the sticks over the dowels to hold the window open and push cotter pins through the dowel holes to secure the sticks *(below, bottom)*.

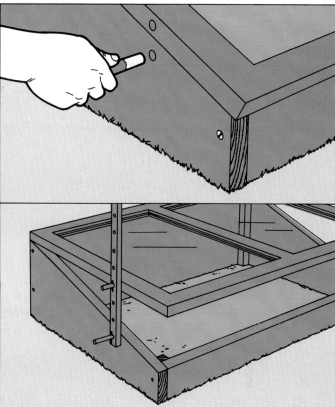

Tips for Using a Greenhouse Kit

The easiest, most economical way to add a full-scale greenhouse to your property is to buy one in kit form. Kit models range from compact units, 4 feet by 6 feet, to structures that enclose areas as large as 1,000 square feet.

The least expensive kits contain parts for lightweight redwood structures that rest on a level bed of sand or gravel and are covered with plastic film. Somewhat more costly are heavier redwood frames that are anchored in the ground and support rigid fiberglass panels. While not crystal-clear, these synthetic coverings admit almost as much light as glass.

Modern glass-paneled greenhouses, built with aluminum frames, are considerably more expensive than wood-frame models, but the aluminum-and-glass greenhouses are attractive and long-lasting and, like wooden ones, can be equipped with automatic climate-control and ventilation. They do, however, require a firm and level foundation, especially in regions of loose soil or heavy frost.

Start the foundation by digging a rectangular trench and pouring a deep footing of concrete *(pages 54-56)*. Build the foundation up to grade with ce-

ment blocks. Then attach the base of the kit to the blocks, using the hardware supplied by the manufacturer.

Almost all greenhouses need devices to keep the temperature within a limited range. Greenhouse manufacturers and garden-supply stores sell heaters, coolers and automatic ventilators but you can keep heating and cooling costs down by locating your greenhouse with its long axis running east and west, ideally underneath a large deciduous tree. This will keep it cool in the summer but give it full winter sunlight, when the leaves have fallen and the sun is low.

4 A Roomy All-purpose Structure

If your car lacks shelter, if your basement is cluttered with tools and garden equipment, or if someone in the family needs a studio or workshop that will not fit in the house, the best solution may be a large outbuilding that can serve almost any purpose except as living quarters. With the help of a few ingenious professional techniques, you can set up a handsome structure that will make life easier for you and increase the value of your property. A turned-down slab *(pages 106-111)* eliminates the need for costly forms or masonry skills; precut stud walls *(pages 112-117)* can be built on the ground and erected as a unit; and prefabricated trusses *(left),* which require no tricky rafter cuts or ridge beam, make the installation of a sloping roof a simple assembly process.

When planning a substantial structure of this type, consider the requirements that its use will create. A garage needs a driveway route, walkways, a turnaround and perhaps a side door as well as a main entrance. If you plan to store garden tools in it, you will want a door that provides easy access to the garden. A studio or shop should have windows, and you may want a loft for storage. If you will need electricity and water, consult your local utility companies about preparing the structure for their installation.

Draw a floor plan of the building on a map of your property to make sure it is located at least as far from the house and the property lines as the local code requires. Then sketch front and side views of the building on graph paper to determine whether the building will harmonize with the main house and surrounding property. You may wish to plan the roof pitch and overhang of a new structure to match those of the house or of other outbuildings. If you suspect that the building may interfere with a prized view or block sunlight essential to the well-being of a garden, you can check by hanging a series of sheets on lines stretched between poles to create the effect on your property that the building will have.

You will probably need a building permit. Bring along your diagrams and sketches and be prepared to describe the type of foundation, wall construction and roof design that you propose. Some localities require a test of the soil to determine whether it will support the proposed structure. And set up an inspection schedule well in advance so that work will not be delayed.

Make a list of materials needed for each of the three stages of the job—foundation and slab, stud-wall framing and roof framing—and arrange delivery times that will mesh with your working schedule. If you order all the materials at once for staggered deliveries, you can usually get a contractor's discount—which may sometimes reduce the cost of the building materials 10 to 20 per cent.

A Special Slab Combining Floor and Foundation

For a sizable building, the simplest base is a turned-down slab—a concrete slab, cast as a unit around a skeleton of reinforcing steel and wire mesh, with its edges turned down into trenches. The turned-down rim supports both the slab and the walls above it, and protects the slab from frost heaving. The builder need not pour conventional footings or lay a foundation wall of concrete block, since both footings and foundation are provided by the rim.

This slab's most distinctive feature, its turned-down rim, is also its main limitation. The rim requires trenches not much wider than the blade of a shovel, but deep enough to meet footing requirements for your area. Digging a trench that meets these specifications may be impossible in regions where frost penetrates deeper than 2 feet. Even digging to 16 inches, the minimum necessary for strength, may be difficult in sandy soil. If your local building department advises against a turned-down slab, use a deep concrete footing and block wall similar to those described on pages 54-58.

In all likelihood, you will need the advice and consent of the building department on other aspects of the slab and the building that rises above it. Most communities demand a building permit for any structure large enough to need a turned-down slab, and require that outbuildings be located a minimum distance from property lines and from the main building. Generally, before you undertake to pour a large slab, you must submit to your building inspector a rough map of your property, showing the main building and proposed addition.

To prepare for construction, plan an expedient route for the heavy trucks that will be bringing in building materials and concrete. Make the delivery spot as close to your building site as possible.

On the job itself you can save time and work more effectively with rented professional tools. A transit level enables you to establish lines and angles quickly and accurately. A power tamper will help you compact the soil before the concrete is poured; a power troweler will speed the job of finishing the concrete. You will also need a cutter and a bender for rebar—steel reinforcing bars *(page 27)*—and a 50-foot tape measure.

The slab on the following pages has a flat floor. To make a drainage slope for such buildings as garages, use forms at the door openings to form a slope of 1 inch in every 8 feet from the back wall. String lines and drive grade spikes between the door forms and the back and side walls to shape a drainage trough that channels water to flow out of the doors.

Laying Out the Forms

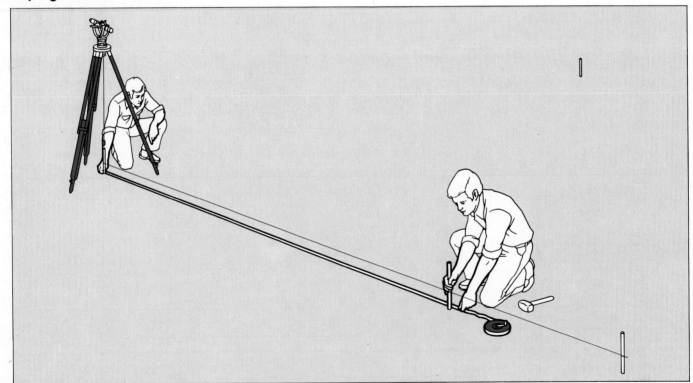

1 **Finding the building lines.** Drive stakes to mark the two corners at one side of the slab. Use a transit level to set a third stake at a right angle *(page 12)*; string a line to this stake from the stake beneath the transit, and measure along the line with a tape to locate the third corner. Drive a stake there, set the transit above it and repeat the operation to find the fourth corner. Run a boundary of string about 4 inches off the ground around all the corner stakes.

2 **Building batter boards.** Drive three 2-by-4 stakes about 2 feet outside the strings at each corner and nail 1-by-6 boards, each 5 feet long, to the stakes to form a right angle; set the tops of the boards about 10 inches above the ground. (A sledge hammer or a large brick makes a solid backing for nailing.) Drive a 1-by-2 sighting stake a few inches outside each set of batter boards so that the sighting stakes stand slightly higher than the batter boards.

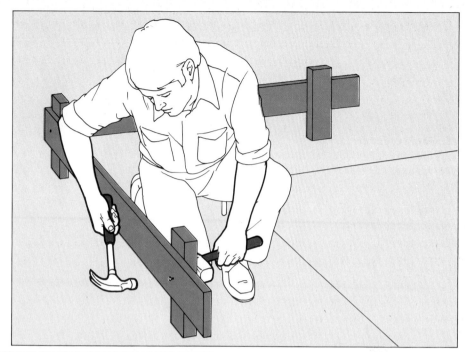

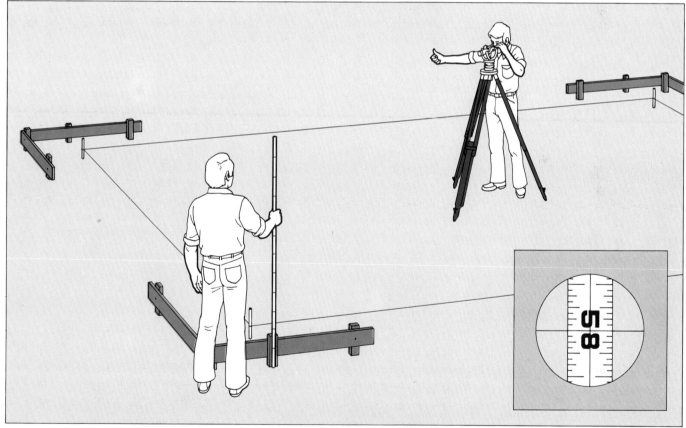

3 **Leveling the batter boards.** Place the transit at the center of the building site and have a helper hold a 6-foot ruler next to one of the sighting stakes outside the batter boards. Level the transit, sight through it at the ruler and note the measurement seen—in this example, 58 inches (inset). Subtract 8 inches from the reading. At each sighting stake, have your helper raise the ruler until you see this calculated figure in the transit, then mark the sighting stake at the bottom of the ruler. Drive the batter-board stakes down until the board tops meet the marks on the sighting stakes; lay a level on the board tops to see that they are even. String lines between the batter boards directly above the lines that run between the corner stakes (Step 1).

Remove the corner stakes and strings, and grade the area between the batter-board strings to a flat surface 8 inches lower than the boards (pages 15-16). Tamp the soil thoroughly.

Building Turned-down Slabs

1 **Placing level forms.** For each section of forms, nail three 16-inch 2-by-4 stakes to an 8-foot length of 2-by-8. Set the inner face of the forms along the string lines and drive the stakes into the ground until the top of each form is level with the string line. Nail the forms together at the corners and nail an 8-by-12-inch plywood backing between stakes at the points where the form boards butt together.

2 **Setting grade stakes.** String lines between the back- and front-wall form boards every 4 feet. Then drive ⅜-inch reinforcing-bar spikes along the strings at 4-foot intervals, with the tops of the metal spikes level with the strings.

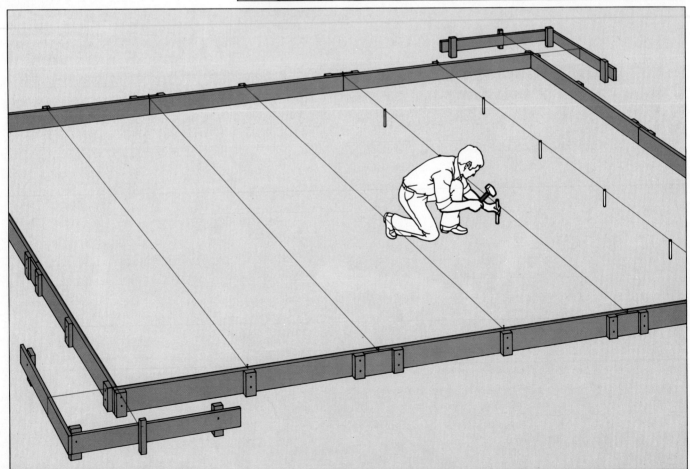

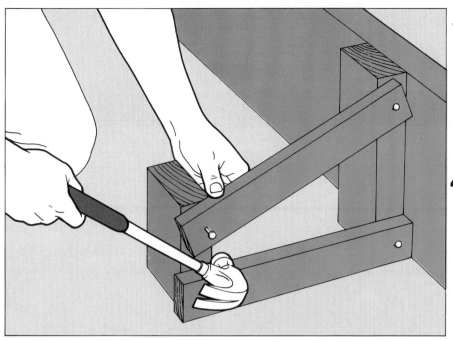

3 **Bracing the forms.** Drive a 2-by-4 bracing stake a foot behind every form-board stake. Nail two 1-by-2 braces between each bracing stake and form-board stake, one on the ground, the other diagonally. To prevent concrete from leaking out between the forms and the ground, shovel a layer of dirt or gravel behind the forms.

4 **Digging the trenches.** Along the inner face of each form board dig a trench 12 inches wide and as deep as is required for footings in your area. Bevel 5 inches from each inner edge.

Every 4 feet along the trench bottom, drive a pair of ½-inch reinforcing-bar spikes about 5 inches apart into the trench bottom, with their tops about 5 inches below the form top. Set a brick flat on the ground next to every pair, and lay two lengths of horizontal reinforcing bar on the bricks against the vertical reinforcing bars.

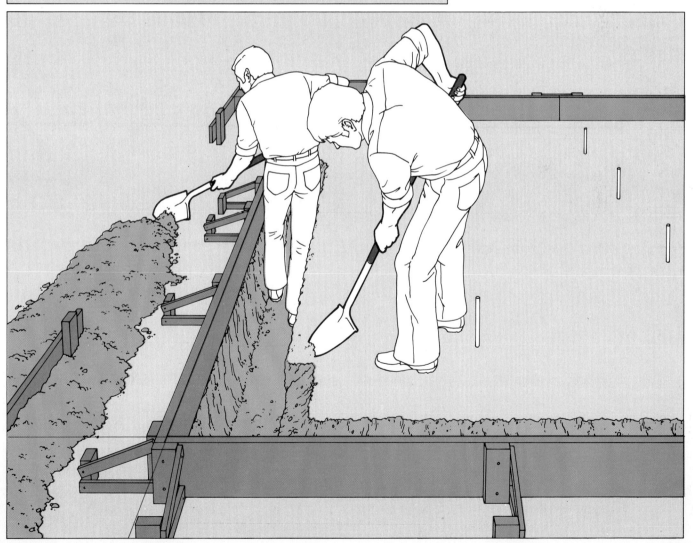

5 **Interlocking the steel.** Wire the horizontal reinforcing bars to the vertical ones about an inch from the tops, and wire the horizontal bars together at the trench corners.

Spread a 3-inch layer of clean 1-inch gravel over the main part of the building site—do not let any gravel fall into the trenches—and cover the gravel with sheets of 4-mil polyethylene. Over these sheets lay down 6 × 6–10/10 wire mesh extending almost to the form boards, and wire the edges of the mesh to the reinforcing steel.

Prepare sole plates of pressurized lumber for installation (*Step 7, below*) by drilling ⅝-inch holes every 5 feet and 1 foot from each end of a 12-foot length of 2-by-4. Prepare enough sole plates to extend around the rim of the slab.

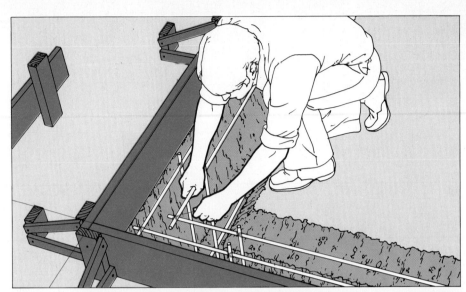

6 **Filling the forms with concrete.** Enlisting several helpers, pour and spread the concrete, tamp it into the trenches with a piece of 2-by-4 and, using a rake, pull the wire mesh a couple of inches up into the slab. Level the surface with a screed of 2-by-4s, making the concrete even with the tops of the form boards and the grade spikes. When it is level, drive the spikes below the surface of the concrete. Finally, smooth the concrete with a darby.

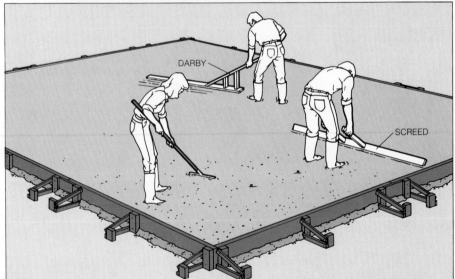

DARBY

SCREED

7 **Installing the sole plates.** Run ½-inch anchor bolts 12 inches long through the holes in the sole plates, fit each threaded bolt end with a washer and a nut and set the plates on the wet concrete, ⅜ inch in from the form boards. Work the bolts down into the concrete, tapping the threaded ends with a hammer if necessary. Make sure no bolts are installed in door openings.

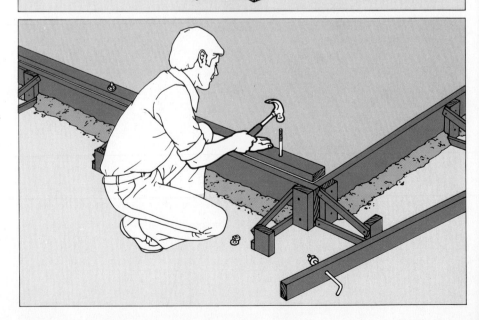

8 Finishing the slab. When the concrete is hard enough to walk on but still visibly damp, finish the surface with a power troweler. Set the blades flat against the surface and run the machine over the slab, then readjust the blades to angle upward and smooth the surface by running the machine over it again.

Sprinkle the concrete with water, cover it with sheets of polyethylene and let it cure for 3 days or more before you remove the forms.

Grade Beams: Stiffeners for a Concrete Floor

Concrete is a strong building material, but if a slab is poured on marshy soil, clay or a site that has been leveled with fill, it may settle and eventually crack. When building over poorly compacted soil, many professional masons reinforce a slab with grade beams—trenches filled with concrete and reinforced with steel. The beams serve much the same function as the wooden beams that support the floor of a house.

The grade beams shown at right are the type generally used with a turned-down slab. They are poured in trenches 8 inches wide and 8 inches deep, spaced every 4 feet between the slab-rim trenches. Half-inch reinforcing rods are laid over bricks set on gravel, then wired to the reinforcing bars in the rim trenches. Then another layer of bricks and two more reinforcing bars are set in and the slab is poured as a unit.

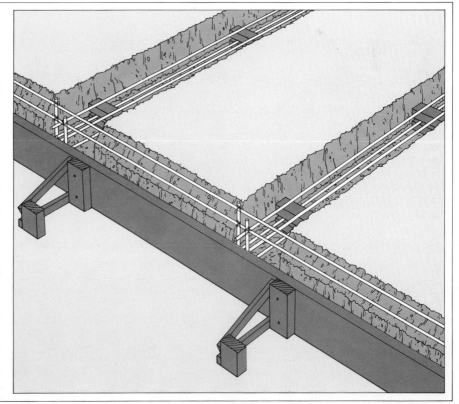

Sturdy Walls Nailed Flat and Tilted Up

Stud walls provide a sturdy framework suitable for any structure, from a shed to a house. The principles of stud-wall construction have been standard ever since sawmills began trimming lumber to uniform dimensions: vertical studs spaced evenly are nailed to horizontal top plates, each wall is tilted upright section by section and the studs are toenailed to a sole plate. At each opening the roof load is carried by a horizontal header—generally a board-and-plywood sandwich 3½ inches thick—that is supported at its ends by posts or studs. The method is the same for any large structure—a garage *(below)*, a workshop with windows and a side door, or a capacious barn with a loft.

To prepare for a job of this magnitude you will need to draw a rough set of plans, to show to the building inspector when you apply for a building permit and to refer to as you work. Start by drawing a simple floor plan on graph paper; indicate the overall dimensions of the structure, which walls the roof will bear on, the distance between the center of each opening and the nearest corner of the building, and the size of each rough opening (usually specified by the manufacturer of the finished door or window).

Then draw head-on views—what architects call elevations—of the walls that have openings; indicate the height of the walls, the height and span of each opening and the sizes of the studs, posts and headers that will support the roof.

Use the plan to determine exactly what materials you need when you order lumber. Studs—generally 2-by-4s precut 8 feet long at the sawmill—are usually spaced 16 inches apart, although some local codes permit 24-inch spacing. The 2-by-4 top plates should be straight pieces of structural-grade lumber at least 14 feet long; shorter pieces or warped lumber will make the wall sections difficult to align. The headers in a nonbearing wall can be made from lumber as small as 2-by-6, but for long spans in bearing walls you will need structural-grade 2-by-12s. If you want a single large door rather than the small ones shown below, you can use a header reinforced with a long steel plate ½ inch thick—but you will need a brawny crew to lift it, because it will weigh more than 20 pounds per linear foot; in some localities you will also need heavy posts with special footings to support such a header.

Precision is important in constructing exterior walls because they support the entire roof. When you mark stud locations for two parallel walls, you should start the layout for each from the same end of the building; the walls will then be mirror images of each other and the roof will bear evenly on them. Make sure the rough openings and the spacing between studs are correct—a minor layout mistake can cause huge problems once the walls are up. And take pains to plumb the walls accurately and brace them firmly. The temporary braces must hold the entire structure rigid while the roof trusses are put in. When the roof has been sheathed, remove the braces one by one as you apply the wall sheathing.

You can build a large structure with ordinary household tools, but a few professional ones will ease the work. You can use a colored, waterproof lumber crayon to highlight penciled layout marks outdoors. The 16-penny nails this type of construction requires can be driven more easily by a 20-ounce claw hammer than by one with the standard 16-ounce head. And you can use a heavy brass or steel plumb bob to check the corners of the walls, rather than trying to shield a lightweight bob from the wind.

How the walls fit together. In this typical two-car garage—a rectangle 24 feet by 20 feet—the horizontal sole plate is fastened to the foundation by anchor bolts *(page 110, Step 7)*. The studs are nailed to the sole plate and to the lower layer of top plates; the second layer of top plates is nailed to the first to tie the walls together at the corners and at the joints in the first layer. Temporary diagonal bracing holds the corners plumb until the roof and wall sheathing are installed; braces nailed to stakes hold the walls in line with the corners.

The continuous 2-by-12 header, spanning the two 8-foot door openings and the wall between them is easier to install than independent headers for each opening. The 4-by-4 posts that support the header hold it tight against the top plate, so that no spacers or short cripple studs are needed. Horizontal 2-by-4 fire stops nailed between the studs are required in some localities; they add rigidity to the structure and provide a nailing surface for exterior sheathing.

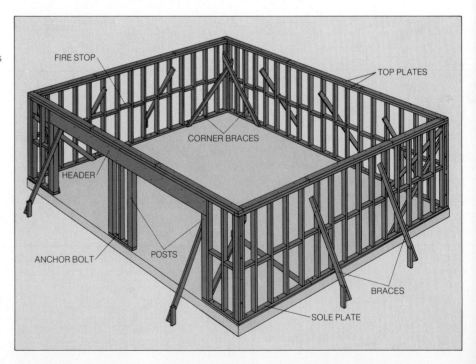

Preparing the Plates

1 **Marking the bottom plates.** Drive a nail partway into the bottom plate of one of the side walls, 15¼ inches from the outside edge of the back corner. Hook a long tape measure over the nail and have a helper hold the tape taut on the sole plate. Hold the 1½-inch-wide tongue of a framing square perpendicular to the plate with its front edge against the nail, draw a line across the plate on both sides of the tongue, and mark an X between the lines. Mark the sole plate this way every 16 inches all along the wall, holding the front edge of the tongue to the 16-inch interval marks on the tape measure.

Lay out studs for the other side wall in the same way, starting from the same end of the building; similarly lay out the back wall and the two front walls that are outside the door openings.

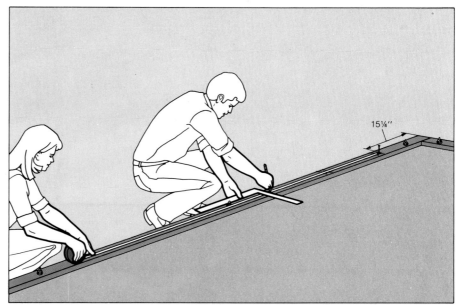

2 **Laying out the top plates.** Have a helper hold one of the top plates against the sole plate so that their ends line up at the corner. With the framing square, transfer the layout marks made in Step 1 to the top plate. Then mark across both plates at the center of the last stud mark on the top plate; cut off the top plate along the mark, so that the joint will fall directly above a stud, and line up the next section of top plate with the mark on the bottom plate.

Transfer layout marks to the remaining sections of top plate in the same way; when you reach the corner of the building, make sure the last section of top plate is at least 8 feet long and cut it off in line with the end of the bottom plate.

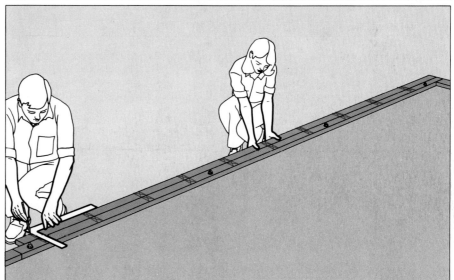

3 **Laying out the garage doors.** Measure from the outside edge of the sole plates at the front corner to locate the center of each garage-door opening; then measure from the center line to locate each edge of the opening exactly. With a handsaw, cut off any portion of the sole plate that extends past the edge. To lay out the opening for the garage doors, draw lines across the sole plates at either side 3½ inches from the edges of the opening and mark Xs on the sole plates for 4-by-4 posts. Draw a line across both the top and sole plates an additional 1½ inches back and mark an X on each for the full-length studs that will run alongside each post.

At the center wall between the two openings, mark an X for a 4-by-4 post at each end of the sole plate and for a stud between them (*inset*).

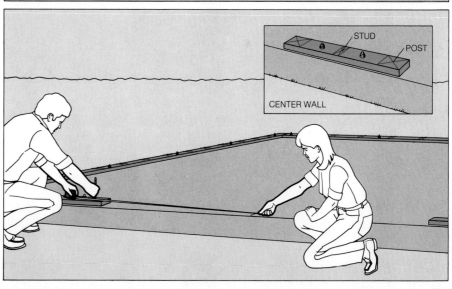

Raising the Walls

1 Nailing the wall together. Set studs on edge near each layout mark on the bottom plate of one wall and set the top plate above them with its layout marks facing the studs. Line up each stud with a layout mark on the top plate, hold it in place by standing on it and drive two 16-penny nails through the plate into the stud.

If a stud is located at a joint in the top plate, make sure only half of the plate bears on it and angle the nails toward the center. If a stud is laid out over an anchor bolt, notch the bottom end of the stud to fit over the bolt.

2 Preparing the corners. Sandwich three 2-by-4 blocks between two of the straightest studs you can find, making sure the blocks line up with the sides of the studs and do not protrude beyond their ends, and fasten the sandwich together from each side with 16-penny nails. Nail this corner post to the end of whichever top plate runs past the adjacent one at the corner *(inset)*. To complete the corner, nail another straight stud to the end of the adjacent top plate when you assemble the adjacent wall. The stud will be nailed to the post to tie the two walls together.

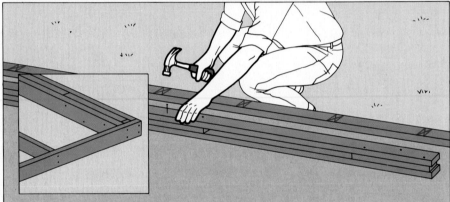

3 Tilting the wall upright. With one helper for every 8 feet of wall, lift the top plate from the slab and tilt the wall upright. Set the studs on the marks on the bottom plate, check with a carpenter's level to make sure the wall is roughly vertical and brace it every 6 feet with long 2-by-4s *(page 76, Step 3)*. Toenail each stud to the bottom plate with 10-penny nails, two from one side and one from the other.

Lay out and erect the other side wall and the back wall in the same way.

4 Posts to support the header. Nail together the two front walls on the slab, using top plates that hang over the door opening at least 3 feet. Then fasten 4-by-4 posts to the studs nearest the door with staggered 16-penny nails every 10 inches. To determine the length of the posts, subtract the 1½-inch thickness of the sole plate from the height of the rough opening specified by the door manufacturer. Erect and brace the front walls *(Steps 1-3)*.

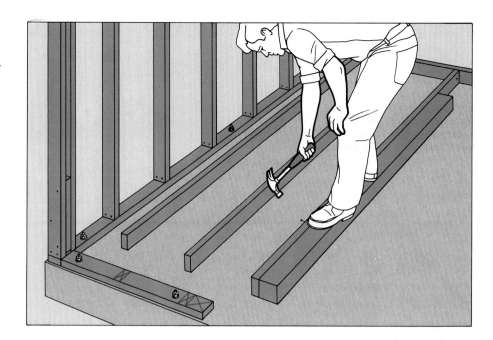

Aligning the Framework

1 Plumbing the corners. Drive a nail partway into the top of the top plate near the corner stud and dangle a plumb bob from the nail, with the tip of the bob level with the top of the bottom plate. Make a temporary brace by cutting 45° angles on both ends of a long 2-by-4. Rest one end of the brace on the slab next to the sole plate of the adjoining wall and nail the other end to the side of the corner stud near the top plate of the wall you are plumbing; make sure the brace does not protrude beyond the stud. Remove any temporary braces near the corner and have a helper move the wall gradually toward the vertical. When the tip of the plumb bob lines up with the edge of the sole plate, have a second helper nail the bottom of the corner brace to the sole plate of the adjoining wall.

Move the plumb bob to the other side of the corner and brace the adjoining wall in the same way; then brace the other corners.

2 **Lining up the walls.** Temporarily nail a 2-by-4 block to the side of the top plate near each end of a wall. Drive nails partway into the top plate behind the blocks and stretch a string tightly between the nails, using the blocks as spacers to hold it 1½ inches out from the top plate. Use a scrap of 2-by-4 as a gauge to measure the gap between the taut string and the top plate at each brace; have your helpers unfasten the brace from the stud, move the wall until the string barely touches the block and nail the brace securely to the stud. Line up the other walls in this way.

2 × 4 SPACER

3 **Adding the second top plate.** Place a 2-by-4 plate on top of the original top plate, starting at a corner where the top plate of the adjoining wall runs through to the outside edge. One end of the new plate should overlap the original top plate of the adjoining wall; cut the other end so that it falls at least 4 feet away from joints in the lower top plate. Nail the new plate to the lower one with staggered 16-penny nails, one between every pair of studs. If the new plate is not straight, force it into line with toenails angled through its side into the top of the lower plate.

To tie the corners together, have your helpers push the studs of adjacent walls toward the corner; when the original top plates meet, drive two 16-penny nails through the end of the new plate into the old top plate of the adjoining wall.

Install the other new top plates in the same way, lapping the joints between the lower plates and tying the corners together *(inset)*. Then nail the temporary corner braces *(page 115, Step 1)* to every stud they cross.

Bridging Large Openings

1 Building the header. Measure between the layout marks for the studs on either side of the garage doors and cut two straight 2-by-12s to this length. Cut strips of ½-inch plywood 11 inches wide to match the length of the header. Apply a thin, zigzag bead of construction adhesive and set the plywood strips on the 2-by-12, the short piece in the middle. Apply construction adhesive to the plywood and set the other 2-by-

12. Nail the sandwich together from both sides, with staggered 16-penny nails 10 inches apart.

If your header will not be supported by a center partition, build the sandwich around a ½-inch steel plate. Have your supplier drill holes in the plate and use the plate as a template to drill the 2-by-12s. Fasten the sandwich together with ½-inch machine bolts with washers *(inset)*.

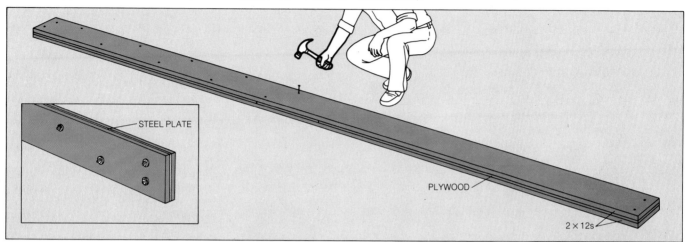

STEEL PLATE

PLYWOOD

2 × 12s

2 Lifting the header into place. With one helper for every 5 feet of header length, lift the header and slide it onto the posts. Have the helpers hold the ends in place while you nail the stud alongside the post to the header end and nail the top plate to the top of the header, using 16-penny nails. Fasten the header to the post, stud and top plate with framing anchors. If the header does not fit snugly against the top plate, nail a plywood spacer or short cripple studs on top of it. Finish the top plate with a length of 2-by-4 and add a second top plate *(page 116, Step 3)*.

3 Building the center wall. Cut two 2-by-4 posts and one stud to fit tightly between the header and the sole plate of the center wall. Set the posts and stud in position and toenail them to the sole plate. Check one post with a level, adjust it until it is perfectly vertical and toenail it to the header. Measure between this post and the other at the sole plate, transfer the measurement to the bottom of the header and make a layout mark there; do the same for the stud. Toenail the post and the stud to the header, then fasten both of the posts to the header with framing anchors.

Ready-made Trusses to Support the Roof

The fastest and cheapest way to frame a roof for a simple rectangular structure is to use premanufactured trusses. They eliminate the need for heavy structural joists and rafters, for the tedious cutting of rafters at complex angles, and for the dangerous job of erecting a ridge beam.

The modern truss, based on building techniques that go back to 2500 B.C., resembles the ones widely used for the wooden bridges of the 19th Century. It is composed of three principal timbers, called chords: two top chords that form the slope of the roof and a bottom chord that spans the distance between the exterior bearing walls. The three corners of a truss are joined with metal or plywood gussets. Additional members, known as webs, are fitted between the top and bottom chords to support the top chord and transfer stress to the bottom chord and to the exterior bearing walls. This design feature helps prevent the walls from bowing outward.

Because the average truss for a 20- to 30-foot span is made of 2-by-4s, it can be lifted into place with little effort, and a whole roof can be completed in hours—a job that might take days with traditional framing methods. And because these standardized prefabricated trusses can span as much as 40 feet without center supports, they provide unencumbered interior space by eliminating the need for interior bearing walls.

When ordering trusses, you need to specify the span between the exterior walls of the building, the length of the overhang and the type of end cut—plumb or square—that you desire. You must also specify the pitch of the roof. The standard pitch for trusses spaced at 24-inch intervals is 4 inches to 1 foot but local codes in areas with heavy snowfall may require a greater pitch or more closely spaced trusses. Consult your local building inspector or truss manufacturer for this information. If the pitch of the roof is not regulated by code, trusses that match the pitch and overhang on your house generally give a pleasing appearance to your new structure.

Order the two end trusses with webs spaced 16 inches apart so that sheathing can be nailed to these trusses before they are put up *(page 121, Step 6)*. And have an opening framed in the end trusses so that you can install a ventilator.

Trusses come in a variety of styles. If you plan to build a catwalk above the bottom chords for storage, order a truss that has no center web, rather than the type shown on these pages. If you are planning to store heavy objects on such a platform or hang objects from the trusses, order heavy-duty trusses.

To erect trusses, you will need two adjustable scaffolds 6 feet high, available at most rental agencies. You will also need two framing anchors *(page 78, top)* for each truss and a large supply of galvanized nails. Trusses rely on sheathing rather than the traditional ridgepole for stability. Buy enough ⅜-inch tongue-and-groove weatherproof plywood to cover the roof—use ½-inch to ⅝-inch plywood in areas of heavy snowfall—allowing 10 per cent extra for waste. Buy 1-by-6 lumber—two 8-foot-long sections for every three trusses—which you will use to hold the trusses in place until the sheathing is installed *(page 122, Steps 4-5)* and then will reuse to space the bottom chords of the trusses *(page 124, Step 3)*.

You will need at least three helpers to lift and roll the trusses into place. When lifting the trusses, always carry them in a vertical position with one worker at each end and another in the middle to support the bottom chord.

Preparing the Walls and the End Trusses

1 **Marking positions for trusses.** Standing on a scaffold, use a steel tape to measure 24¾ inches from the side wall and make a mark square across the front wall's top plate. Put an X and a second line on the side-wall side, to indicate the exact position of the truss.

Lay out the rest of the trusses on 24-inch centers, using the first mark as a starting point. Then lay out the other wall, starting your layout from the same side wall. If the trusses are properly laid out, every second truss should fall directly over a stud in a wall like the one shown here.

2 **Fastening the framing anchors.** Place the framing anchors on the top plate so that their raised edges align with the marks on the top plate. Nail the framing anchors to the top plate with eightpenny galvanized nails.

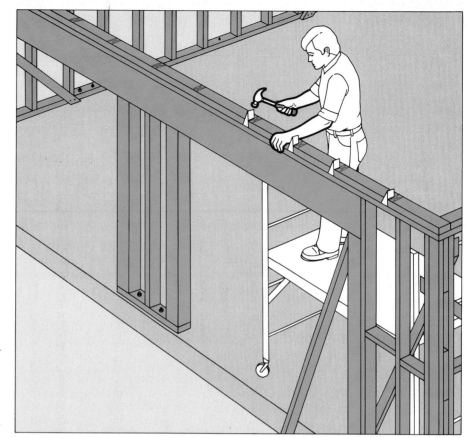

3 **Laying out the overhang.** Overhang is not essential but improves appearance and weather protection. Nail 2-by-4s long enough to provide the desired overhang, to the outside faces of the top plates of the side walls, and flush with the tops of the top plates. Mark the length of the overhang from the front wall on each 2-by-4, then tie a string line tautly between the marks.

4 **Fastening the nailer.** Nail 8- to 10-foot
lengths of 2-by-4 over the top plates of the side
walls and flush with the outward edge of the
front wall. Space them 1½ inches from the outside edge, using a 2-by-4 block on edge to
maintain the 1½-inch spacing while nailing.

Prepare the "scabs"—bracing—for the end
trusses by cutting 4-foot strips of sheathing and
nailing them to four 8-foot studs (inset).

SHEATHING

8' STUD

5 **Erecting the scabs.** Nail two scabs (Step 4, inset) to each side wall, about a third of the way in
from the front and back walls. Position each
scab so that the top edge of the sheathing is flush
with the top plate of the wall and the rest of
the scab sticks up above the top plate far enough
to provide support for the end truss.

6 **Sheathing the end trusses.** Lay the end truss-es on the ground and cover them with 4-by-8 sheets of plywood, aligning the short edge of the plywood with the heel and bottom chord of the truss. Snap a chalk line along the top chord of the truss and the heel and then cut the plywood along the chalk line. Nail the sheathing to the truss. Similarly finish sheathing the truss. Cut a ventilator opening with a saber saw.

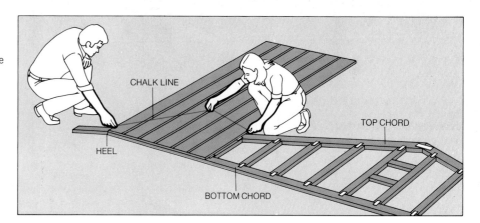

Raising the Roof

1 **Hoisting the end trusses.** With two helpers, carry an end truss upside down into the building and from a scaffold lift one end until the top chord rests on the wall plate. Then, with a helper standing on another scaffold, set the other end of the truss atop the opposite wall plate.

2 **Rolling a truss.** With two helpers on scaffolds holding the truss in position, wedge a 2-by-4 into the peak of the truss and rotate the truss into an upright position.

When the peak is upright, walk the truss over to the side wall and set it between the 2-by-4 nailer and the scabs. Align the overhang with the string line on the front wall and nail the scabs to the top chords of the truss.

3 **Securing the end truss.** Standing on a ladder outside the building, drive a 16-penny nail through the sheathing and into the truss and nailer.

Roll the second truss up, align it with the string line and secure it to the top plates by nailing it to the framing anchors on the wall plates.

4 **Bracing the top chords.** Nail a 1-by-6 to the end truss, its end flush with the outside of the top chord. Align the second truss at a distance equal to the truss spacing, mark the brace and nail it to the truss. Nail another 1-by-6 brace on the other side of the ridge.

5 **Bracing the remaining trusses.** Roll up, anchor and brace all the other trusses except the last four, bracing them as you go. Attach the remaining end truss. Roll the last three trusses up, then walk them into place and secure them.

Completing the Job on Top

1 **Plumbing the end truss.** Nail a 16-foot brace made of 2-by-4s between the ventilator framing of the end truss and a 2-by-4 stake firmly anchored outside the building. Loosen the scabs and adjust the brace while a helper plumbs the end truss with a 4-foot mason's level. When the truss is plumb, nail the brace to the stake.

Set up the scaffolds along the side walls and, with a helper, snap chalk lines along the upper chords of the trusses 4 and 8 feet from the overhang to lay out the plywood sheathing.

2 Sheathing the trusses. Tack the corners of a 4-by-8 piece of plywood to the end truss, its edge flush with the outside edge. While a helper re-checks the end truss for plumb, tack the corners of the plywood on the center line of the fifth truss. Nail the plywood down with sixpenny galvanized nails spaced every 6 inches.

After sheathing the bottom 4 feet of the roof, remove the 1-by-6 braces and sheathe the next 4 feet, starting the first sheet of plywood 4 feet from the end truss so that joints will overlap.

3 Stabilizing the trusses. Connect the bottom chords of all trusses by nailing to them the 8-foot lengths of 1-by-6 bracing that you removed from the roof. Align the chords with the marks on the bracing *(page 122, Step 4)*, so that the bottom chords are spaced exactly as far apart as the top chords. In high-wind areas, nail additional 1-by-6 diagonal braces to the webs between the top chord of each end truss and the bottom chord of the fifth truss from each side wall.

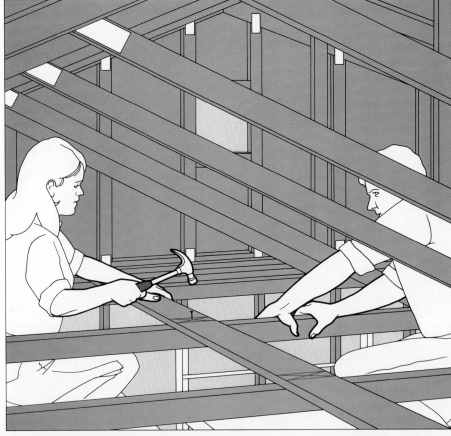

Sheathing with Plywood Panels

For a simple outdoor structure like the one shown on the preceding pages, you can save time and money on sheathing and siding by using sheets of exterior-grade plywood 4 feet wide to serve as both. Manufacturers now make plywood in a variety of textures and simulate all but the most intricate siding patterns.

You can get this type of paneling in 8-, 9-, or 10-foot lengths; when ordering, make sure you specify an exterior-grade plywood, made with waterproof glues. If you are setting your studs 24 inches apart, make sure the plywood is the extra-thick kind designed for this spacing. If you plan to set the panels against the studs horizontally, put blocking between the studs 4 feet from the bottom of the wall to serve as a nailing surface.

To make sure that the panels are watertight, use a Z-cap flashing between the end-truss panels and the side-wall panels. Then use sealant *(Step 2)* to caulk between the panel joints unless you use panels with special tongue-and-groove or shiplap edges. Protect the corners of the building with corner molding and use galvanized nails to prevent rust stains.

1 **Nailing the sheathing.** Slip a Z-shaped piece of flashing *(inset)* under the back side of the truss panel and then hold a full-length plywood panel under it while a helper nails the panel to the studs. Put nails every 6 inches around the edges of the panel and every 12 inches along the intermediate studs. Continue attaching the plywood panels in this fashion, butting them over the studs but leaving $1/16$-inch vertical gaps between them to allow for expansion.

2 **Weatherproofing the siding.** Caulk the gaps between the plywood panels with a polyurethane or silicone sealant. Cover the exposed edges of the plywood at the corners of the building with strips of right-angle corner molding *(inset)* or, if you prefer, simply butt lengths of 1-by-3 and 1-by-4 lumber at the corners.

Picture Credits

The sources for the illustrations in this book are shown below. The drawings were created by Roger C. Essley, Fred Holz, Joan S. McGurren and Jeff Swarts. Credits for the pictures from left to right are separated by semicolons, from top to bottom by dashes.

Cover: George de Vincent. 6: Fil Hunter. 8 through 13: Walter Hilmers Jr. 14 through 19: Peter McGinn. 20 through 25: Frederic F. Bigio from B-C Graphics. 26 through 31: Walter Hilmers Jr. 32: Fil Hunter. 34 through 39: Nick Fasciano. 40 through 49: John Massey. 50: John Massey—courtesy of New-York Historical Society. 51, 52, 53: Eduino J. Pereira. 54 through 60: Walter Hilmers Jr. 61, 62: Eduino J. Pereira. 63: Raymond Skibinski. 64: Library of Congress. 65: Nick Fasciano. 66: Fil Hunter. 68 through 73: Peter McGinn. 74 through 77: Frederic F. Bigio from B-C Graphics. 78: Nick Fasciano. 80, 81, 82: John Massey. 83, 84, 85: Raymond Skibinski. 86 through 89: Eduino J. Pereira. 90 through 93: Gerry Gallagher. 94, 95: Frederic F. Bigio from B-C Graphics. 96 through 99: Peter McGinn. 100, 101: Gerry Gallagher. 102, 103: Margaret King. 104: Fil Hunter. 106 through 111: Peter McGinn. 112 through 125: Frederic F. Bigio from B-C Graphics.

Acknowledgments

The index/glossary for this book was prepared by Mel Ingber. The editors also thank: John Agnew and Ray Fox, The Good Earth Nursery, Falls Church, Virginia; Bamboo and Rattan Works, Inc., Hoboken, New Jersey; Anne Bendann and H. Gerard Ebert Jr., Innerspace, Inc., Baltimore, Maryland; Joseph Berchielli, Tech Components, Beltsville, Maryland; Berrall-Jasper Fence Company, Inc., Washington, D.C.; Donald Blevins, Ed Detwiler and Al Ozuna, Virginia Concrete, Springfield, Virginia; Briner's Rental Service, Oxon Hill, Maryland; Clifford H. Brown, Hallmark Iron Works, Newington, Virginia; John M. Brozena Jr., Accokeek, Maryland; J. H. Burton & Sons, Olney, Maryland; California Redwood Association, San Francisco, California; Jere Cessna, Belaire Service Company, Bowie, Maryland; Chicopee Manufacturing Company, Cornelia, Georgia; George Clark and Roy Weaver, Devlin Lumber and Supply Corporation, Rockville, Maryland; Morris Coffin, Coffin and Coffin, Washington, D.C.; Alfred Copeland, Copeland & Kephart Civil Engineering, Alexandria, Virginia; Robert Dinsmore and Carl Fenton, Flippo Construction, Washington, D.C.; Wilbert Eller and Richard Thomas, Dale Lumber Company, Falls Church, Virginia; James R. Elliott and Glenn Halme, American Plywood Association, Tacoma, Washington; The Fence Works, Vienna, Virginia; Sally Fennell, Burson-Marsteller, New York City; Dr. Lelland T. Gallup, Cornell University, New York City; John Gattuso, Design Resource Associates, Reston, Virginia; Stanton W. Gedvillas and John Liebl, The Yeonas Company, West Vienna, Virginia; Robert Gerber and David Jacobson, Fairfax City Building Authority, Fairfax, Virginia; Harris Gitlin, Cooperative Extension Service, U.S. Department of Agriculture, Honolulu, Hawaii; Glawe Manufacturing Company, Dayton, Ohio; Harold Hartman, Los Angeles, California; Floyd Harvey, Floyd Harvey Masonry, Inc., Washington, D.C.; Kenfair Manufacturing Company, Alexandria, Virginia; John Koehlein, Portland Cement Association, Arlington, Virginia; Van Lane, Preferred Construction, Leesburg, Virginia; Ernest Muehlmatt, Springfield, Pennsylvania; Reggie Nearing, Laurel, Maryland; D. R. Norcross, Timber Engineering Company, Washington, D.C.; Jim Papile, The Woodworkers, Alexandria, Virginia; Lee Peterson, Cedar Fences, Inc., Upper Marlboro, Maryland; Popular Science, New York City; Ken Porter, Building Group, Inc., Washington, D.C.; Quality Way Fence Company, Alexandria, Virginia; Paul Schoellhamer, Washington, D.C.; Roger Smith, American Rental Association, Moline, Illinois; Ed Stolda, Standard Supplies, Inc., Gaithersburg, Maryland; Frank Trinca, C. M. Peletz Company, Burlingame, California; J. M. Turner, University of Georgia, Athens, Georgia; R. E. Yeck, U.S. Department of Agriculture, Beltsville, Maryland.

The following persons also assisted in the writing of this book: Ellen Cramer, Jane Colihan, Sarah Harrison, Henry Wiencek and Bill Worsley.

Index/Glossary